HOW TO
not
SUCK
as a
CHRISTIAN

JEREMY STEELE

Copyright © 2025 by Jeremy Steele; First Edition; Printed in the USA
Cover design and interior layout by Matthew J. Distefano

PAPERBACK ISBN 978-1-964252-33-9; HARDBACK ISBN 978-1-964252-34-6; ELECTRONIC ISBN 978-1-964252-35-3

 QUOIR

Published by Quoir
Chico, California
www.quoir.com

CONTENTS

FOREWORD   VII
By Brian D. McLaren

INTRODUCTION   XI
Do You Suck?

1. Take the Bible Seriously Not Literally   1

2. Good Christians Doubt   11

3. Be Pro Choice Because God Is   21

4. Don't Talk to People That Way   35

5. Don't Preach on Street Corners   47

6. Don't Manipulate People Into Giving You Money   55

7. Stop Defending Your Faith (Apologetics)   63

8. Don't Make God Small Enough to Agree with You   75

9. Stop the Homophobia   83

10. Stop Asking Kids to Sign Purity Pledges   107

11. Respect Atheists, They Are Doing Ok   119

12. Choose Beliefs, Don't Inherit Them   127

13. Believe That God is Love   137

14. Racist Leaders Have to Go   149

15. It's Time to Stop the Camp Alter Calls   155

16. Know What the Bible ACTUALLY Says About Hell   163

17. Believe Science   175

Books and Other Stuff You Should Check Out   185

To all the people I have hurt when I sucked as a Christian

FOREWORD

By Brian D. McLaren

You may have brought someone to tears. It may have been a family member, a friend, a colleague, or even a complete stranger.

You quoted a Bible verse or spouted some clever line you heard on a religious/political radio/TV show or online video. You were trying to be a good soldier, a loyal member of your religious army.

But when you saw the tears, you thought, "Is this the kind of person I really want to be? Am I happy with what I'm becoming?" You felt concerned enough that you picked up this book.

Or maybe you didn't. Maybe you doubled down and told them they needed to repent and that you were only "speaking the truth in love," and if they don't like it, it's their problem.

Maybe you even went on TikTok or Instagram to share your "wisdom" with others. Maybe years passed and you began to enjoy making people cry, or making them angry, or getting them to call you names.

Maybe, when people told you that you were being too harsh or judgmental, you told yourself that Jesus was persecuted and rejected for his obedience, and now you're following in his footsteps by putting people in their place ... as sinners, as heretics, as a liberal woke mob, or whatever.

So maybe over time you went from hurting a few people in Jesus' name to hurting many. And maybe you became arrogant and mean-spirited in the process.

And so here you are right now, finally having second thoughts. You can't tell your Christian friends about your second thoughts, because then they'll suspect you of "conforming to the world" or of "catching the liberal woke mind virus." They'll put you on a prayer list and before you know it, other people will be quoting weaponized Bible versus against you just as you have done to so many others.

Having others do to you as you have done to others? When that happens, the whole process doesn't feel so good or seem so holy.

Whatever path brought you here, you have picked up this book by Jeremy Steele, and the title resonates with what you need.

Wouldn't it be nice if a book like this weren't needed?

I'm not just speaking about other people needing this book ... wouldn't it be nice if I didn't need a book like this?

The fact is, many of my greatest regrets across my whole long life have to do with ways I have harmed people not in spite of my faith but because of it.

Because I was trying to be a "good Christian," I hurt people. And of course, in doing so, I hurt myself as well, because we are all connected. (There are Bible verses that prove that, but most Christians prefer to quote different Bible verses that give them permission to hurt others in Jesus' name, or in the name of love or truth or Scripture or whatever.)

In one of my recent books (*Do I Stay Christian?*) I wrote, "Nobody is born a religious jerk. It takes a religion to help someone become that way."

In picking up this book and in daring to turn its pages, you are on your way to facing some ugly truths about yourself ... ways you have been a religious jerk, ways you have sucked at being a Christian.

And facing ugly truths about ourselves is a beautiful thing. It takes courage. It also takes grace. And that's the combination you'll find in these pages.

Jeremy Steele has walked this path himself, so he speaks with grace. And he knows how desperately, even violently, people defend their delusions of spiritual superiority and religious over-confidence ... so he combines that grace with courage.

The world already has more than enough religious jerks, and each day, more sincere people are recruited to the cause. What the world needs now is for more and more of us religious jerks to experience a change of mind and heart. (Some of you know the Greek word used in the Bible for that kind of deep change!) This book is a superb resource to help in that process.

It combines honesty with humility. It combines common sense with research. It combines careful thinking with compassionate feeling. It might unsettle you and a few chapters might even make you angry. But if you don't throw the book against a wall and walk away in a huff, I predict you will soon find yourself saying, "Thanks, Jeremy. I needed that."

There are many books, talks, sermons, websites, radio/TV shows, and internet influencers who will help you suck more at being a Christian.

But this book by Jeremy Steele—along with his amazing array of free online posts—will help you suck less.

And if the word "suck" bothers you, don't you think being a religious jerk should bother you more?

INTRODUCTION

Do You Suck?

There is a strong possibility you suck as a Christian.

I say that because I do and have sucked as a Christian.

I am an expert.

In my experience (especially on TikTok), the more confident you are that you don't suck, the more likely it is that you actually suck as a Christian. Before we go any further, we need to pause for a couple of seconds because sometimes people don't track with very old slang... like sucking.

I'll never forget being called into a meeting with my senior pastor (I was working with teenagers in a church at the time) because a mom accused me of cussing and speaking vulgarly during my sermon to the teens the week before. I walked into the office, and she was sitting there, glaring, lips pursed and legs crossed, ready to watch me squirm.

"Jeremy, Ms. Leah has some concerns," My pastor began. (this was also in the South, where women were routinely demeaned by giving them Ms. and their first name to make sure they knew where they fit in the social structure). "She said you used a choice word or two during your sermon this week."

At this point, I literally had no idea what she was talking about. I racked my brain. I hadn't said anything that approached inappropriate as far as I could remember.

Don't get me wrong, I cussed, just not professionally.

I prodded, "What was the word?"

"Well, I'm definitely not going to say it," She responded.

"I don't think I said anything close to inappropriate. Can you give me a hint?"

The pastor looked at me and said, "You used the word 'sucked.'"

I was baffled. "I'm sorry. I don't understand. How is that inappropriate?"

She exchanged a meaningful glance with the pastor and then said. "It refers to a sex act."

I threw up a little in my mouth hearing her say that. "What? No.... I didn't..." I looked at the pastor for support. "That's not what it means. It means something is, like, bad. No one thinks of it as *that*."

The pastor interjected, "Well, at least one parent does..."

You can imagine the rest. Suffice it to say that is not what I mean when I use that term in this book. When I talk about you (or me) sucking as a Christian, I mean nothing sexual and everything about our theology, reading of the Bible, and the way we act in the world about God.

So, why do you have this book?

If someone gave this to you, it's fair to say they may have thought you suck as a Christian (also they may just know you love snarky theology). Don't be offended; they have given this to you be-cause they want you to do better, they think you are smart enough to be able to read, AND they respect you enough to think that you might be able to both read AND change.

As far as I am concerned, the biggest miracle we get to see in this world is real, meaningful, positive change in other people. And whoever gave you this book thinks you are one of the rare people capable of that miracle.

But maybe you bought this book for yourself. In that case, bravo! You are likely starting one step ahead.

Somehow you have been able to accomplish a feat that is almost unheard of in the modern world: self-reflection.

You have been able to be honest enough with yourself to realize that you aren't perfect, that you might be wrong, and that you, likely, suck in some way at being a Christian. And to be brutally honest, you are probably right.

You probably suck.

And I definitely suck.

But when you start there, you can be sure you are on a journey (I'm contractually obligated to use that word since I have over 100K followers on a social media platform) toward positive change. And not just change in yourself, but being an agent of positive change in the world. If there is anything I think Christianity should be, it's an agent of positive change in the world, and that doesn't happen through an ideology. It happens through people, but be careful.

There is a real danger in these pages.

The words here can hurt. I'm serious. When someone calls out a place where you suck, it hurts. I know that well. Just before I sat down to write this part of the book, another video went viral on TikTok and about three thousand people told me I was wrong, evil, and going to hell.

Those used to hurt, but the scar tissue really helps.

However, along the way in reading and responding to those comments, about ten people pointed out some places where I actually got it wrong and genuinely sucked. Those hurt because they were true.

For most of us, that kind of exposed pain makes us recoil. Our default response is to protect ourselves from the pain by pretending we were right when the pain is trying to tell us that we suck in this area.

And that's the danger in this book: the recoiling.

Don't let it happen.

When some of the words in this book make you recoil, when they resonate in that vulnerable place do your best to stay there, to stay open. Let me be clear: that may be the most challenging thing anyone can ask you to do, to remain present with pain. But that's where the good stuff is. That's where you begin to really see yourself and shift into a better place.

When you feel the instinct to recoil, stop. Look up. Feel what's going on and make a decision. Consider what it will take not to recoil. Consider what it will take for you to be able to avoid entrenching yourself in the suckiness. You may need to keep reading (after taking a couple of deep breaths). Or you might need to put the book down for a bit and take a walk to think. Or, maybe you leave that chapter for a minute and go on to another one. Do what you need to do.

Just don't recoil.

But that brings us to an important question, what's going on in this book and how do you use it?

What follows in this book is a list of things that people often suck at as Christians, things that make people who are not Christians (and many who are) cringe and run away. These are things that make people hate the church, Christians, and God. They are things we need to stop (or start in some cases).

Though there are threads that weave throughout the whole book, each chapter stands on its own so feel free to bounce around from chapter to chapter. (How arrogant is it to think that I can tell you what to do with this book?! It's yours. Ignore me; I'm just the machine that tried to make words that help people change.)

At this point, I must say that though the content in the chapters is my own, the list is not mine. It is a combination of roughly a hundred ideas that my followers on TikTok suggested for this book. Many of them are not Christian, some of them are atheists, all of them are hoping this book will help you not suck.

Also, I want to own that I am a middle-aged white man who lives in the United States of America. There's not a lot I can do about that except own that and all of the ways in which it has given me privilege and bias and all the things.

I grew up in the racist south of the 1980s and 1990s and spent a lot of my career as part of evangelical megachurches in a mainline protestant denomination. Though I would love to imagine a world in which I could let go of all of that and write from a place of complete objectivity, that is not possible. So, know that all of the stuff that sucks about all of that is definitely going to come through in these pages. I will work hard not to fall into the pits that life has set up along my path, but I know I won't see them all. When you find one, let me pre-apologize.

I'm sorry. I suck.

But because I only know my own context well enough to really speak honestly, that's where I'm writing. Though everyone is welcome to read these pages, I am assuming most of them are in the United States and at least care in some way about religion, spirituality, or making the world a better place. If that's not you, welcome and I'm sorry for the times it feels like you are sitting in a room where I am talking to someone else.

Lastly, I am going to give you a Bibliography of books/thoughts from other people that inform each chapter. Though I put them at the end of the book, they really are some of the best stuff in here. I hope you'll eventually work through all the books in that bibliography because they are all amazing. I can't say I agree with every word of the works referenced. Still, they are the things that helped me find my suckiness in this book and it seems only fitting to give them the credit.

So, congratulations. You suck.

Now, let's do something about it.

1

TAKE THE BIBLE SERIOUSLY NOT LITERALLY

The Bible kind of sucks. Ok, maybe not the best word, but it's complicated.

On so many different levels.

What makes the Bible suck is the way that Christians have used and abused it over time. Over the centuries it has been used to justify holy wars, slavery, the oppression of women, minorities, queer people, you name it.

Part of the problem is that the Bible was written thousands of years ago to cultures that don't exist anymore in a country/region that currently less than 1% of the world's population calls home. Yet it is the sacred text of billions of adherents that have spanned over 2,000 years and the entire globe. With that kind of diversity and history it is bound to be a complete mess. Sometimes it's a beautiful mess, but it's always a mess.

When you look back at all the ways the Bible has been weaponized and used for horrible violence, there is one rule that rises above the rest. One rule that if everyone would follow, we might avoid some of the worst paths.

Take the Bible seriously, not literally.

How I Suck as a Christian

I was thirteen.

I was carrying my "sword of the spirit," as I had taken to calling my Bible at the time, in school and opened it up before my science class to pick up reading where I left off. It was 1 Corinthians 14. I had never read this passage, and I was about to really suck as a result. When I got to the end of the chapter I read:

"Women should be silent in the churches. For they are not permitted to speak but should be subordinate, as the law also says. If there is something they want to learn, let them ask their husbands at home." (1 Corinthians 14:34-35 NRSVUE)

I paused and remembered all the times this had been violated in my church. There were literally women allowed to talk everywhere. In fact, the person who taught our middle school youth group was a woman. And this verse said they should be silent! I didn't understand. I also knew my mom would be pissed if I said anything about this to her because, well, to put it politely,

My mom was a liberal school teacher.

But, at the same time, the bible literally said it. I was going to follow what it said, and things were about to get messy. After school I went to a Bible study and there was a girl there who spoke up and when she was finished I raised my hand and asked a question.

"I read today that women are not allowed to talk in church and should ask their husbands to teach them instead. Does that apply to girls too?"

I can't believe I'm sharing this right now, but it's just proof of my expertise in sucking. The person leading the Bible study didn't jump down my throat or agree with me (thankfully). They asked where I read it, and we all turned to read the section from 1 Corinthians. Then my leader explained that there was more to this verse than meets the eye. The teacher talked about how it appears that in this specific church in the city of Corinth, they had a problem that the writer was addressing. It wasn't meant to be a universal rule because, in other parts of the Bible, this same writer encouraged women leaders.

I was off the hook, and my mom never knew... until now.
Sorry mom.

But this is the problem. A literal reading of the Bible can be disastrous. Let me rephrase. A literal reading of the Bible HAS been disastrous and continues to be disastrous.

We need to take the Bible seriously, not literally.

Because the Bible is so complex and layered, its most profound meanings are rarely on the surface. They seldom exist in the literal meaning. Instead, reading the Bible as your sacred text requires that we let go of focusing on reading it like an instruction manual (seriously, if I hear one more evangelical use that metaphor I am going to COMPLETELY LOSE IT).

Instead, we need to engage it in serious conversation or study or a better word that combines those two. There's a metaphor people like to use when talking about the Bible that might be useful as we think about it. A lot of Christians will say something like the Bible is alive. Or quote that verse, saying that it is living and active, and sharper than any two-edged sword. I love that.

The Bible is alive.

It's perfect partially because it's not unique. Really all texts are alive. When we read Shakespeare or Rowling or King or Stoker or the Dalai Llama, the text only has meaning as it is read. And that meaning is created in each reader's brains as their synapses develop connections between the words and their understanding of language.

The meaning emerges from this soup of memory, bias, and a definition you learned in the third grade. It isn't ever the same for everyone. Right now, as you read these words, you might be still in a midsummer night's dream, Diagon Alley, Pennywise's sewer, Dracula's Castle, or a Tibetan temple because your brain latched onto a name in that list.

(I'm in Diagon Alley, by the way. And yes, I know she is problematic for LGBTQ people, but her books also have changed the modern world possibly as much as the Bible, so she is part of the human canon).

The Bible is like that. It comes alive in our brains and souls and hearts and grows there. And allowing that to happen is one of the best parts of engaging with it. When we treat it as a living thing, we can engage with it seriously without assuming we actually control it or can entirely understand it.

Reading it is like spending time with your beloved grandparent who says very inappropriate things sometimes, they love you and want to help you be the best version of yourself, but they are kind of racist. Or actually racist, or maybe not because you can't fully understand what is going on under the surface because racism seems to be entirely opposite of your grandparent's character.

That's the Bible. Our weird, possibly racist grandparent who we are pretty sure is a good person at their core.

By this point, most of you know I'm going to hell for talking about the Bible like this, so why stop now?

But how do we get anything out of it?

How do we let it help us form our beliefs and become the best versions of ourselves if it's living, unpredictable, and sometimes hard to understand?

We take it seriously.

By looking at all the layers, trying to find their original meaning, and then trying to find a correlation to our modern lives, we discover the deeper meaning.

Or

We read it and enjoy the quirkiness as we look for the places where it causes more love, peace, and inner connection to grow within us, where it helps us feel like we are connecting with the universe and being transported into some state of divine union. (I'm allowed to talk that way because I lived in Northern California for a while.)

But if you aren't just reading for the quirks and love, let me talk to you about some things to consider when you are trying to engage in more serious study. First, the Bible has a TON of different genres of literature in it. You will find poetry, history, allegory, myth, legal documents, battle body counts, and weird apocalyptic prophecy that feels like sword and sorcery fantasy.

And sometimes, there will be multiple genres in the same chapter.

For me, genre is a good starting point because it helps me get an overall sense of how the original writer and audience would approach it. If it's poetry, they are looking for meanings in between the words and hidden under the metaphor. If it's history, they are trying to form meaning from things that happened and discover who they are from who they were. You get the idea.

From genre, I move to culture. This is really important. Culture is a tricky little domain because culture is often like the air we breathe. It's there, we use it, but we never really think about it or name it until something changes about it. But culture changes. Cultural values change, and those values shape the definition of words. Take a moment to think about all of the things that are culturally defined and change over time:

Marriage, Sexuality, Rights, Food, Death, the Afterlife, Art, Taboo Topics, Beauty, Scandal, Style, What it means to be Free, Health, Parenting, War, Law, Historical and Academic Values.

That last one was a setup because I want to say something about it. Historians in the ancient Near East had different values regarding history. They felt that the best history told the truth of what happened from the events.

Accuracy was not the highest value; truth was.

If you told the story exactly as it happened but the meaning was unclear, modern historians would say you did an excellent job, while ancient historians would say you did a bad one. That's because the cultural values around history have changed. This means when you read two accounts of the same battle in the Bible that are different, it's not because they aren't accurate. It's because the historians are trying to accomplish something different in the ancient world than in the modern one.

When you read a specific passage you want to study, a good first task is identifying the genre. Then, take a moment to ponder what elements are present that may be informed or defined by the ancient culture.

Once you have identified the cultural elements, think about what your modern cultural values are around those things and do a bit of digging through reputable resources (check out the Bibliography) to learn about what the ancient cultural values were and how they differ. Once you have those things, you can begin to piece together what the meaning might be for the original writer and readers.

But there's a huge aspect we left out that can deeply affect a passage's meaning. I left it out because most people shouldn't attempt to deal with it: the ancient languages. What you are reading when you read the Bible is most likely a translation from Hebrew, Greek, and/or a little Aramaic into your chosen language. All translations are not created equal and one of the worst is the King James (it was translated in the 1400s and we have discovered so many more ancient manuscripts and understand those languages so much better now).

The academic consensus is that the New Revised Standard Updated Edition is the best English translation for study.

Unless you are considered a Biblical scholar and do peer-reviewed articles in academic journals, you have no business breaking open a Hebrew Bible and googling the word you find.

Don't do it.

I have graduate-level training in ancient Hebrew and Greek, and the main thing I learned is that I have no business translating them myself. I know how to read and use the tools created by people who actually know what they are doing. If you haven't completed several hours of coursework in ancient Hebrew and Greek, find a scholar you like (I like Dan Mccellan on TikTok) and let them do the ancient linguistic work for you.

How do you do all of this? Don't worry, we are going to practice this together. We will be working a whole lot of stuff out around the Bible and by the end you'll get the hang of it!

Last and most certainly not least, don't just base your beliefs on the Bible. You need more. I think, at the very least, your beliefs need to be formed by the Bible, things that other smart people have said, things your spiritual family members have taught you, your own experience, and LOGIC. Seriously, logic.

There's a whole chapter on this too.

This is a much harder way to approach the Bible, but like with most things, the harder way often yields much better results.

2

GOOD CHRISTIANS DOUBT

When you asked questions that challenged the dominant narrative about the Bible in the religious circles I grew up in, you were dismissed or silenced. Instead of serious engagement and searching for answers, the reply was almost always some version of, "You just have to accept that on faith," or like one pastor said to me, "You don't want to be a doubting Thomas." More on that later.

They just silenced you. That was the response. Well, unless it concerned evolution, then they brought out creation pseudoscience to make sure you learned to distrust the academic institution and science in general. If you pressed the issue, you got pulled aside after Sunday School and reminded that you were risking being welcome in that community. "You know, when you keep asking questions like that, you are causing others to fall away from the faith." Which was code for "If you keep doing this, we are going to encourage other people to not talk to you because you are sowing seeds of doubt in their minds."

How I Suck as a Christian

Enter my high school self. My skeptical mind was coming into its own while I was still being brainwashed by evangelicalism. I had memorized a bunch of Bible verses and knew all kinds of things I was supposed to believe about everything from abortion to homosexuality, but I wasn't as sure as everyone said I should be. I had doubts.

I felt guilty for doubting.

Well, I felt guilty when I wasn't feeling morally deficient for being unsure about God or Jesus or whether or not there was a fish big enough to swallow a human whole. But I knew very well that doubting was not ok.

I was hard on myself.

I beat myself up for questions. I tried to ignore them and never, ever ask them. Ok, sometimes I did, but I added that to the things I would beat myself up about.

And, of course, as a good fundamentalist, I didn't keep that inside. I enforced it on the others around me. I remember sitting at a lunch table in my high school with other Christians and shaming them for doubting while dismissing their questions with answers that were meant to silence instead of inform.

I sucked in part because I was following the example of other pastors I had seen.

I have watched pastors say that you need to get rid of the people in your life that cause you to doubt, that cause you to not be firm in your beliefs. And after the pastor rebukes you in public, people stop talking to you. They stop inviting you to hang out or go to the movies. Little by little, you slip from the center of the community to the sidelines and finally out the back door.

That's why it isn't a surprise when I get messages from followers on TikTok saying they are afraid to doubt. They are concerned that they will lose contact with their families, that their friends will reject them, and that they will be completely alone as they process their unraveling faith.

Ultimately, many of them turn to scholars and religious leaders like me online to help them process their doubts because saying their doubts out loud to the people they love could risk every-thing.

And that's a problem because, as far as I can tell, good Christians doubt.

Like, think about some of the recent Christian allstars, you know, the people who no one would say weren't on the right path of Christianity. People like Mother Theresa, the nun who spent her life serving some of the poorest people in the world in the streets of Calcutta, India. This paragon of faith and social justice had deep moments of doubt at one point, writing in a letter, "The place in my soul is blank. There is no God in me." Even people famous for their philosophical and theological arguments for Christianity doubt. C.S. Lewis, Martin Luther, John Wesley, and so many others wrote about their (oftentimes multiple) seasons of serious doubt.

But, if you are like many of us who are recovering from some form of evangelicalism, you still feel a need to make all your beliefs square with the Bible, or at least to make some sense of the Bible. As strange as it may sound, for me, it was the Bible that helped me break free and be comfortable with doubts.

The Bible taught me that doubt was a good thing.

It taught me this lesson when I was in one of my deepest seasons of questioning. As usual, I was beating myself up over not accepting things on faith, as I had been told over and over again. This particular time I was replaying what that pastor said to me a long time before, "You don't want to be a doubting Thomas," when I realized I had never actually paid attention to that story.

So I got out my giant study Bible, looked up the story in the concordance (index) in the back, and started reading John 20. This is the part of the Jesus story that happens after he dies but before he ascends into heaven. It begins by noting that all the disciples were gathered in one place but that one of the disciples, Thomas, was not with them.

That would be "doubting Thomas."

As soon as it mentioned that detail, I knew why. I knew how Thomas was feeling. If he was anything like me, he had completely lost his faith when Jesus died on the cross.

I started to connect with Thomas. If he was a skeptic, a doubter like me, the beginning with Jesus had to have been really difficult. It was likely hard for him to accept all the hype about Jesus being the Messiah. It must have been a stretch for him to believe that Jesus was actually healing people or raising people from the dead.

Then, little by little, over his three years of following Jesus around, Thomas started to believe. He began to risk thinking that it actually might be true. I imagine that at some point, Thomas went all in on believing that Jesus was who everyone else believed he was. Then, over the course of a couple days he saw Jesus get brought up on false charges, convicted, and then executed as a common criminal.

How could Thomas have been so stupid? So gullible?

How had he let go of his reason and become one of those irrational religious people?

Yet, he saw all the people around him who still believed, who were holding out hope for something to happen. These were the people he had spent the last three years with, his friends, the people he loved and cared about most deeply in the entire world.

And he knew that the thoughts he was having would crush them.

He knew that he could eviscerate their beliefs with a couple of sentences.He knew that if he did that, it would take the last little bit of wind out of their sails. And he couldn't bear to do that to them, especially after what had just happened.

So, he left.

He opted out.

Not because he didn't need them, but because he couldn't bear to hurt them. That's why Thomas wasn't there.

I mean, that's why I wouldn't have been there if I were Thomas.

While all the disciples (sans Thomas) were gathered in a room behind a locked door, Jesus appeared like the video you had been longing to see in your For You feed. The same Jesus they had seen die on a cross days before was standing in the room. He said, "Peace, be with you..." and spent some time hanging with them.

After all of that happened the disciples rush over to Thomas. They tell them about the miraculous appearance of Jesus.

Thomas was having none of it.

He said that they are OK to believe whatever they want to believe, but he needs proof. He will require data. He will need to put his fingers in the nail holes to believe that Jesus is actually back. He's not going to be duped again.

Then, some time passes, and it appears that the story is starting over. It says that the disciples were in the same room with the door locked like before when Jesus appears again. Jesus begins with the same words "Peace, be with you..." It's all the. exact. same. except for one thing:

Thomas is with them.

Whatever they said about Jesus appearing to them didn't convince Thomas to believe, but it did convince him to rejoin his friends.

And when this resurrected Jesus is standing there in the room with Thomas, re-doing the whole interaction, Thomas doesn't let up. He doesn't demur and say, "Oh lord, forgive me for doubting." No. No self-respecting doubter would do that. Thomas stands firm. He demands data. He demands the proof he needs.

And Jesus response? Does he try to silence his doubts like my Sunday School teachers when I was a kid? Does he passive-aggressively threaten to leave him out of the community like the pastors I was around? No. Jesus gives Thomas the proof he needs. Jesus answers the questions and encourages him to believe.

That story shook me.

If I am completely honest, it still does. Because the doubts were honored and given space to be expressed. Someone took the questions seriously and helped guide the questioner to discover answers. And, when the questioner felt like they didn't belong, when they left their friends, the friends told the doubter that they belonged in the community with their doubts and questions.

Doubts didn't didn't disqualify them from the community.

Any religious community (or person) that is trying to follow the way of Jesus will never silence or shame people for having doubts and questions.

But I want to go a step further. If Jesus didn't shame Thomas for doubting, we shouldn't feel in any way negative about having doubts. I think that Jesus' honoring of Thomas' doubts indicates that the very thing that one might feel excludes Thomas is a path to faith and connection with God.

In other words, good Christians doubt.

The longer I live, the more I realize that doubts aren't a symptom of spiritual deficiency. Doubts are an indication of spiritual health. The fact that you are doubting or questioning means that you are thinking deeply about life and faith. You aren't passively believing whatever some random person who claims to know stuff about God says (we often call these people pastors). No, you are listening, considering, and trying to work out whether or not this or that thing is true.

That is spiritual health.

The more you live and consider and study the more you will encounter new ideas. Many times those ideas conflict with convictions you currently have or the beliefs you had been taught. Sometimes, they are a new nuance of an existing understanding. Every once in a while, you'll find a direct echo of your current belief, but in my experience, that is very rare.

When you encounter those new ideas, you can choose totally ignore them.

That's an option.

You can hold to your existing beliefs and not engage deeply with life, information, and the world around you. I have seen people do that. I've done it myself. But that is in no way healthy. That doesn't help you grow.

Ignoring new data is diverting the river that is feeding the lake of your life and turning your lake into a stagnant pond. Yeah, it stops the change brought by all that new water swirling around, but eventually the algae sets in, covers over the whole place, sucks up the oxygen, and starts killing all the beautiful life that the river once brought to the lake.

All of that means that if you don't want to suck as a Christian, you need to start doubting. You need to start questioning, and if this book helps you do that, I'll count myself a success. So, let's go on a journey together (there we go again with the 'journey').

If you're still not quite ready to sing the praises of your doubts, just keep reading.

I'll be Thomas with all the doubts demanding data and you can be one of the other disciples keeping me around because you aren't questioning it all like me but you still aren't 100% sure yourself. Deal?

3

BE PRO CHOICE BECAUSE GOD IS

If there is one thing I can say online to get the most people to tell me I'm going to hell and am a false prophet, it's that God is pro-choice. This debate is interesting because it is such a new one. It seems to be born out of the identity politics of a political shift in America and has been used by political manipulators and pastors alike to whip people up into a frenzy like a pool of piranhas that hasn't eaten in weeks.

On the other side of this, it's wild to watch people who claim to be all about the Bible twist its meaning and cherry-pick verses to limit the bodily autonomy of women and foster hatred and division, but I said, "On the other side of this." That's because I was, of course, once a hard-line pro-lifer. And it started at a young age.

How I Suck as a Christian

Once a year, our church ended a little early so we could caravan to one of the four-lane streets in our town. Before we loaded up, there was always a sermon about the sanctity of life and the evils of a culture that would allow people to kill unborn children. The preacher would talk about the hairs on our head being numbered by god (whatever that meant) and how God knew us before we were born.

Then we would head out.

When we parked at the edge of the Wal-Mart parking lot, Mr. Jones would already be there because he was reserving our space. The back of his minivan was open and piled high with abortion protest signs. I always got the one that was about adoption because I am adopted.

If I had to find a single moment to mark as the beginning of my journey to not sucking as a Christian it would be the moment I realized I had been duped by my church into protesting abortion on the street as a kid.

But I digress. The story is, I used to be pro-life, but then my conservative evangelical seminary convinced me to be pro-choice.

Let's be clear. That was in no way what they were intending to do, but it's what happened. And between you and me, I think I ended up converting one or two of my classmates to the dark side, too.

Halfway through seminary (which is important to note because I had a lot of high-level tools, like an understanding of ancient Hebrew, etc., to work with), I was taking an ethics-type class with a rotating series of debate assignments. When it came to the abortion debate, the professor asked for someone to volunteer to make the pro-life argument and someone to take the pro-choice argument. There were many volunteers for pro-life, but no one would take pro-choice. My classmates said they didn't feel right arguing for something they didn't believe in. I, on the other hand, love a good argument and had no qualms signing up for pro-choice after everyone else said no.

To give you a sense of how conservative the seminary was, the professor felt he needed to protect me from the backlash I might receive. When I agreed to make the pro-life argument, the professor said, "Now, class, I want to remind you that Jeremy is agreeing to make this argument for this assignment. He doesn't believe the things he is saying but is doing this so we can have this very helpful academic exercise." He then said, "Jeremy, I don't want you to hold back. I want you to give a full-throated argument, ok?"

That did not need to be said.

I like to win.

I was not planning on losing, even though I was pretty sure I would say everything I didn't believe. I was pro-life. Remember, I had gone with my church and held anti-abortion signs beside the road several years in a row.

Little did I know I would weather a lot more hate on the other side of this debate on TikTok about 25 years later.

The prep for my debate was a little easier because I knew the pro-life argument church people used. I had rehearsed it at school, arguing with my more heathen friends who dared to be publicly pro-choice in the southeast. It was simple: life began at conception. The argument I had been taught was that because life started at the moment the egg was fertilized, abortion was murder. And murder is not just a sin but a crime. Plain and simple.

I knew the Bible verses in Jeremiah that talked about God knowing us before we were born (that's not exactly what it says), the passage in Psalms that said God knit us together in our mother's womb (a beautiful metaphor to be sure). I knew that to win against the pro-lifers in my seminary classroom, my argument would have to be grounded in the Bible and have an answer to those classic verses.

When I sat down to do my research, I realized that I had never thought critically about this issue before.

It was an inherited belief.

All my life, I had been parroting the talking points I heard from the pulpit. This realization filled me with excitement because I knew I would learn things I hadn't known before.

I started looking at the verses I knew already. Jeremiah 1:5, in the translation I was using (NIV), said, "Before I formed you in the womb I knew you, before you were born I set you apart; I appointed you as a prophet to the nations."

I was surprised.

At first glance, this didn't seem to address the beginning of life, but now that I was reading it, I saw that it appeared to be talking about Jeremiah and not everyone. I did a little digging in the academic world and confirmed it. This was talking about Jeremiah's calling as a prophet. This verse was meant to position him as a sort of super-prophet. It was saying that Jeremiah didn't just learn to be a prophet, but in the words of Lady Gaga, he was "born this way." It's who he was. He was a prophet at the cellular level.

Though you can say it might imply that life begins before birth, it's a pretty hard argument to make because that verse in no way addresses that issue. It's just making a metaphor to underscore how awesome Jeremiah was at propheting (I have a graduate degree in theology so I can make up words like that). I knew I would be able to dismiss this verse as addressing the beginning of life with a simple, "If you are going to base your entire argument on a potential third-tier implication in a text that is talking about something completely different, you are on very shaky footing."

Now, this was getting interesting. So, I thumbed over to Psalms. Chapter 139, verse 13 began with words I had heard quoted a thousand times if I had heard them once, "For you created my inmost being; you knit me together in my mother's womb..." (NIV) Well, that sucked. It looked like there was no wiggle room on this one.

It seemed pretty straightforward.

Then I kept reading. "I praise you because I am fearfully and wonderfully made; your works are wonderful, I know that full well. My frame was not hidden from you when I was made in the secret place, when I was woven together in the depths of the earth. Your eyes saw my unformed body; all the days ordained for me were written in your book before one of them came to be."

That changed everything.

(reading Bible verses in context often does)

This was not nearly as straightforward. The entire context leans into metaphor. It talks about the mother's womb, yes, but then it talks about a secret place and ultimately being woven together in the depths of the earth. I wasn't sure about the secret place, but I was familiar with the Hebrew idea of the depths of the earth.

The depths of the earth (also called "the deep" and sometimes "Sheol") are first mentioned in Genesis 1. Before everything was made, it says darkness was over the face of the deep (a.k.a. the depths of the earth, a.k.a. Sheol), and the spirit of God hovered over the waters. At this point in the ancient Near East, the prevailing wisdom was that the earth was flat and rested on top of pillars and waters that were below it.

The waters symbolized chaos and the unpredictable. When a flood happened, they believed it was the waters of Sheol bursting forth and bringing destruction. This first reference in Genesis suggests that God was holding back the chaos of the deep and creating order out of the chaos.

The person writing the Psalm says that God created us there, in the chaos, in the waters of Sheol. In a sense, the writer is calling back to the Genesis story suggesting that each of us is an example of God creating order out of Chaos. The writer ties together the womb, the secret place, and the deep.

It's a metaphor.

Like, 100% a metaphor. It's so much a metaphor that there are metaphors for the metaphor. I knew my argument immediately. I would say, "This is clearly a metaphor as it strings together multiple images of which the womb is one. It's not talking about biology. It's definitely not making an argument for when life begins."

And if they pushed back, I already had the zinger.

"So, which is it? Were we created in Sheol? Or the secret place? Or the womb? If you choose just one to take literally, you're choosing to deny the other two."

I didn't fully realize it at the time, but I was beginning to slip away from the tried and true evangelical pro-life position.

I was becoming pro-choice.

Now, it was time to go on the search for my offensive. I was pretty sure I wouldn't find any direct support in the Biblical text (I was wrong), so I went first to Biblical culture. I dove in to try and discover when the people who were around when the Bible was being written thought life began.

What I found was fascinating. During most of the time Christians would refer to as happening in the Old Testament, the Jewish people tied life to breath. This idea has its seed in the story of Adam when God creates human life by breathing into sand, but ultimately it was a cultural value not a Biblical stance. They believed that life began when a child took its first breath outside the womb.

Later, there would be some debate about whether it began at "the quickening" when a mother first felt the baby kick (like in the story of John the Baptist jumping inside of Elizabeth when Mary comes for a visit).

Some eventually believed that life began at conception (as much as they could understand conception without cellular biology), but it was never a settled fact. There was never consensus during the time of the Bible or the early church that life began at conception.

I knew that would not be enough. I knew I would have to find some expression of this in the Bible. I need an example of a passage that was based on this underlying cultural idea that life did not begin at conception. So, I dug in. I looked for some law, story, or religious rite that would help. I wasn't sure I could find anything; honestly, I was pretty sure that if there had been something, one of my pastors would have told me. I was wrong.

What I was about to uncover would change everything for me.

The first hint I found was in law in Exodus, Chapter 21, verse 22. It said that if a pregnant woman is injured and it causes a miscarriage, the person who hurt her would have to pay a fine.

That stands out because all of the laws were framed around a core concept:

an eye for an eye and a tooth for a tooth.

In other words, if you do something, the same thing is done to you. If you break someone's tooth, your tooth is broken as a consequence. More importantly, when you kill, you are killed. But when it comes to someone fatally injuring a fetus inside the mother, death is not the penalty. In Exodus, the penalty is a fine. It means that the fetus was treated as property rather than a life.

I wanted another verse. One random law seemed a bit obscure, so I kept looking. That's when I found chapter five of the book Numbers. In this chapter, there is something called a "trial by ordeal." Think of the witch hunts that determined whether someone was a witch by tossing the woman into the water to see if they floated because witches were made of wood. If they floated, they were guilty. Same idea here.

If a woman was suspected of adultery, she was brought to the temple (by the husband, of course... #patriarchy). The priest mixed up something called "the water that brings a curse." Then, the woman would drink it. If she were guilty, it would cause her to miscarry.

And that was it. As far as I could tell, this was God-directed abortion at the hands of the priest. As I dove into the verse a bit more, I saw a range of interpretations. What was translated as "miscarry" in my translation was a Hebrew idiom (like when old people say they "aren't a spring chicken"). Some scholars believe this idiom translates best as becoming barren, while others think it is better rendered miscarry. Either way, it worked for my purposes because whether through miscarriage or barrenness, a fertilized egg is prevented from implanting or staying in the womb and coming to term.

And God directs it.

Game. Set. Match.

When the fateful day came, the professor again gave the disclaimer, letting me off the hook, and asked who wanted to go first.

I asked to be second.

My classmates gave the argument I had heard a thousand times. I gave an argument I had never heard, based on the Bible, showing what I thought indicated God being pro-choice, but at the very least, showing that God definitely wasn't pro-life.

I won.

This was partly because the other side hadn't done a good job of finding counterpoints and partially because the evidence on my side was much more convincing to the class.

Every time I tell this story, there is part of me that cringes because of how much control I gave the Bible. If there hadn't been Bible verses involved, I would have been pro-choice long before because of science and medicine. I would have been pro-choice, just like I am pro-vaccine and pro-antibiotics when I have an infection.

I wish I had flipped from one side to the other because I had such high regard for a woman's bodily autonomy or because I saw the incredible social inequality that exists when this particular procedure is criminalized. I wish I'd been moved by rape victims and all the many tragedies that intersect with this issue. Still, like the many evangelical Christians who were teaching me, I allowed sketchy, politicized, conservative Biblical teaching to blunt my compassion and justify deeply harmful views.

That's really the heart of the matter here.

It's compassion and empowerment.

When I look at the Jesus story and the deep throughlines in Christianity, they always point to love and compassion, empowerment, and social justice. Regardless of what someone says about the Bible, those should be our plumb lines. When someone's interpretation of the Bible violates those foundational concepts, we should hold those teachings at arm's length while we look for an understanding that is in harmony with these core values.

So, if you want to not suck as a Christian, it's time to be pro-choice.

4
DON'T TALK TO PEOPLE THAT WAY

Yesterday was the first day in several months that someone didn't call me a false prophet in the comments on TikTok. It may be because I only read about 100 of the thousand or so that came through, but either way, I'm counting that as a win.

Each day, as I try to help people in comments and DMs discover the beliefs that work for them, the ones that help them find a greater purpose and become the best version of themselves.

I also get blasted.

It's mostly Christians.

They tell me I'm a false prophet.

They tell me I am not going to enjoy burning forever in hell. And, at least one a day tells me that the earth is flat. I generally imagine they are all the same personality type, and that helps. I generally don't respond at all, but it hasn't always been that way. Because I suck as a Christian.

How I Suck as a Christian

My first experience with online comment-driven hate was intense. I wrote an article for a regional newspaper (they're like websites but used to be printed on dead trees). I labored over this piece because I was trying to communicate a very simple idea in a creative way without feeling redundant. I leveraged all of my training and experience in writing at the time to produce something I was genuinely proud of. I was trying to say one thing:

God loves you.

At that point in my writing life, I considered it a masterpiece (I have posted it below with permission). I sent it off to my editor, who replied that she loved it and that it was important to say this. She said she sent it to her daughter, who had stopped attending church, and the daughter wished she lived closer so she could try my church. She told me when it would be posted online, and I set a reminder to check it out and share the post.

I was in a series of meetings when it went live, so a couple of hours passed before I sat down at my computer to check it out. I read through it and was astonished to see it had 100 comments!

I started reading the comments.

I was not prepared. As I began to read, people were writing the most hateful things anyone had ever said about me (and I had been a theatre kid who was in show choir in the southeast in the 1990s).

They said I was going to hell. They said I was causing other people to go to hell. They said my kids might go to hell.

And it hurt.

I was mad. I decided I was going to fire back. I was already formulating responses in my head when I clicked reply.

I had to create a username and password.

You might think that classic internet wrench that was thrown into my pain-fueled rage derailed the process, but no. I was determined. Once I had verified my email address and logged in there was a new comment waiting, "Where is that even in the Bible?"

Oh NO. They. Didn't.

I had been to seminary and had taught like ten million hours about the Bible. You couldn't have picked a worse comment to say to me. I gave it to them with both barrels (within 250 characters) and hit send.

I felt a little better.

I took a breath and thought of the other responses. What might I say to the person about going to hell? I came up with something and refreshed the page. There was a reply to my reply. It said something like, "There's no hate like Christian love. I just wanted some verses. I actually agree with you."

It cut like a knife. I was doing exactly what the other commenters had done to me.

I sucked as a Christian.

It's Not About That

What I learned in that moment changed everything for me. As I reflected on what I had done in the comments, I realized my reply wasn't to him or about his comment. My comment was about all the things that had been said to me in that comment stream and, in some ways, about all the hurtful things people had ever said to me in my life.

I learned that when emotions are involved, THIS is often not about THAT.

Often, when people are awful and hateful online or when you are awful and hateful online, it's not about that. It's not about what is happening on the surface. It's not about

the article

or post

or video.

It's like going to the doctor with a fever. The problem isn't the fever; it's a symptom of strep throat.

So much of the hate online and in comments is a symptom. It's pointing to something deeper. The hate is revealing a sickness that has spread unchecked because people keep thinking it is the problem. What's the problem?

People are in pain.

There is deep pain in much of the world. People have been rejected by their families. People have been abused. People have been told by a pastor they are going to hell because of their sexuality. People have lost their jobs and are on the brink of losing everything. People are lonely.

Here's the most insidious part of the whole issue. When some- one hurts you, and you respond to that pain and hurt them, it feels good in the moment. It feels like a release, but that fades quickly, and the pain is still there. What it does is hurt the other person, who often responds to their pain, and you spiral down into deeper and deeper pain.

The process is so damaging because when you respond to your pain, your goal is not to feel more pain. Your goal was to release that pain. Granted, you thought you were releasing pain onto another person, but you were releasing it.

As it turns out, when you talk to people that way online, you're not taking the dandelion up by the roots and throwing it into their nicely manicured lawn. You are crouching next to the dandelion and blowing as hard as you can toward their lawn. Not only is the dandelion plant still growing on your side, but many of those seeds never made it over the fence.

What You Sow Is What You Reap

It doesn't matter what religion you go to. You'll find the same principle reflected in every one of them. What you put out into the world will come back to you. Some say it will come back to you magnified, but all have this same concept.

The way you act in the world is like seeds being sown into your life and the lives of the other people in the world. When you sow hate, hate sprouts all around you. When you sow deception, your world becomes a forest of falsehood (I kept this sentence in because it made me sound like a celebrity mega-pastor).

If you are trying to not suck as a Christian, this has to be a significant part of where you start. If you want to echo the life and teachings of Jesus, you need to be about working for a better, more loving, more just world.

That is a tall order, but it doesn't have to be intimidating.

Several years ago, I picked up a little bit from a Jewish rabbi. He told me about the story of Moses reading the laws to the people. After Moses finished (in Exodus 24:7), the people responded with a phrase in a particular syntax that seemed in the original language. They say something like "All the words God has spoken to us we will do and we will hear."

We will do,

and we will hear.

It's backward, right? Most English translations take this construction and put it into some version of the people saying they will be obedient. But this rabbi said something different. He said that it reveals something about reality.

We often think that the process of faith is hearing, understanding, and then living out what we understand. But, according to this rabbi, we usually don't understand until we act.

It is in the doing that we understand.

We have to act ourselves into a new way of being.

If you want a more loving world around you, you have to be more loving. You have to sow more love with your words and actions. If you want a more just world, you have to create more justice with your words and actions. It doesn't change by thinking. It changes by action. Or, in the words of Rev. Dr. Martin Luther King Jr.,

> "Darkness cannot drive out darkness;
> only light can do that.
> Hate cannot drive out hate;
> only love can do that."

Empathy, Kindness, or Silence

But when someone hurts you, it's hard to sow love. I get it. Really. I find that my first step has to be empathy. I have to stop and think about what I have been feeling when I want to say something like that.

And I was generally feeling pretty horrible. I was in a lot of pain, and many times, the source of my pain had nothing to do with what I was saying.

When I imagine them acting out of pain, it helps. Sometimes, that enables me to be kind. Sometimes, I can respond by assuming good intentions and answering their hate-fueled question with a real answer. Or their hate-fueled observation with a "fair" or "I have felt the same way."

But often, I'm not *that* good at being a Christian.

Most of the time, the best I can do with that empathy is silence. I can stop the reflexive, hateful response in its tracks and let the comment float by.

And in the real world? When we actually know people and see their faces, we can do even more. We can reflect the empathy back to them. When people we know lash out at us, we can say,

"It sounds like you are going through a hard time; what's up?" or,

"That was much more harsh than your normal response. What else is going on?"

I can tell you that when I have pulled people aside and shown that level of empathy, things have changed. Many of them have opened up about something going on at home, at work, or with their kids away at college. They have said thank you and apologized.

Or not.

Some have doubled down on their anger and been offended by my empathy. So, there's that. But the key is that I go away from the interaction feeling like I didn't add to the hate in the world. I didn't blow more anger dandelion seeds into my own yard, and for that, I can be thankful. I guess what I'm trying to say is:

Don't talk to people that way.

Here's that article that inspired so much hate year ago:

God loves you. No, really. God is crazy about you. Everything good and beautiful and desirable in this world is the voice of God calling out to you with the most important message in the universe: God loves you.

That means, that you probably have heard the voice of God more than you know. Every time you saw a beautiful flower, or smelled the salt air at the beach or felt the warm embrace of someone who loves you, you were hearing God whispering through the salt molecules and photons and hugs, "I love you."

Every time you were intrigued by a scientific discovery or were in awe of a medical cure, you were hearing God say, "I love you."

Every time you wondered at the grace of a ballerina or were in awe of a painting by Picasso, you were hearing the same message, "God loves you."

And the best news? God loves you no matter what—no matter how much money you make, how often you drink alone, how many people you've slept with or how honest you were on your taxes. There is nothing you can do to make God stop loving you.

God loves you just as you are with all your faults and flaws, on your good days and bad. Even when you post an inappropriate rant on Facebook, God loves you. God loves you if you act like you love everyone else or if you say bigoted, hateful things to your family at home.

God loves you if you are a workaholic or alcoholic, racist or pacifist, homophobic or agoraphobic. God loves you if you are Republican or Democrat, no matter who you voted for for president or senator or mayor.

God loves you if you root for the Tide, the Tigers, the Noles, or go on dates during the Iron Bowl.

God loves you if you love God or not, if you believe in God or not, if you worship God or not.

God's love is powerful and pervasive, but it is not passive. God wants to take all the good parts of you, all the successful parts, all the nice and pure parts, break them open and flood your soul with them. God wants to infect your whole life with all the good things God placed within you. God wants to love you into being all the best parts of who you are.

God loves you. Period. Anyone who tells you otherwise is lying.

God loves you so much that God doesn't want you to be alone, which is why for millennia people have been gathering together to remember and celebrate this simple truth. Some call it church; some call it service; some call it something more relevant and cool, but they all do the same thing: express this undying, unconditional, transforming love week after week.

Maybe this year, you can carve out some time to go experience this beautiful love of God in a worshiping community. I hope you will, but even if you don't, God will still love you.[1]

---

1. Used by permission of AMG.

5

Don't Preach on Street Corners

I was sitting outside at a bar/cigar store in Orlando, FL, writing a book about how to minister to teenagers, and was having a hard time concentrating because of the guy on the other side of the street holding an actual bullhorn and yelling about gay people and hell.

No one was standing around listening to him. No one was engaging. Everyone was somewhere between annoyed and angry. I remember looking at the guy, and instead of wanting to go wag my finger at him, I felt compassion. The compassion was because, you guessed it, I have sucked as a Christian.

How I Suck as a Christian

If you've ever wondered how you go from being born to yelling about sin on a street corner, let me tell you because I have walked that road.

Yeah. I have done anonymous, scarring evangelism.

It started when my friend invited me to participate in a spring break training program at his church. The program was to be led by a group called, and I'm not making this up, the "Hell Fighters."

We sat for hours and hours over the next two days, being taught different ways to argue with people. They went into detail about hell and had us close our eyes and imagine burning in darkness and feeling bugs on our skin. They told us that if we were compassionate towards people, we wouldn't want them to suffer like that.

They asked us how difficult it would be to give away 100 candy bars to people and then asked why we would have a more challenging time telling 100 people about Jesus.

Wasn't Jesus worth more than a candy bar?

After three days of this programming, they had a test for us. We were going to go to the local mall and evangelize. We were going to walk up to random people and ask them a simple question:

"If you die tonight, do you know where you would go?

Heaven or hell?"

It was bad. People said all kinds of words to us that we weren't allowed to say in church. They ignored us, and one of them told me they were going to curse me because they were a witch.

I didn't know what to do about that, but they were wearing a Nirvana shirt so I kind of thought they were cool.

After several hours of this, they loaded us up in the church van, took us back to the church, and fed us pizza while we told them about what had happened. They asked if anyone had led a person to Jesus, and one person said they thought they did but wasn't sure. Then they said they were going to take us to a better mission field and said here we should be careful not to fall into temptation but should also look for people who'd had too much to drink because they were more receptive to the gospel.

Then we got on the bus and drove to the strip on the beach.

Evangelism Doesn't Work

Those are extreme examples, to be sure. But the same motivation that flows underneath the guy with a bullhorn and the teens asking strangers about eternity causes your aunt to tell you that you're going to hell for having a tattoo over a heaping plate of casseroles on Thanksgiving.

It's called Evangelism,

and it doesn't work.

Don't get me wrong; I firmly believe in sharing faith with friends and talking about spiritual things with people online. In some ways my entire life online is a version of evangelism. But that's not what people are taught or experience as evangelism.

What you may have been taught in church is that you need to be on a mission to save people from the fires of hell. You need to act like a firefighter pulling people out of a burning building. You likely have been taught that this is compassionate.

It's not.

What happens with this approach to sharing your faith, whether on the street corner or at the Thanksgiving reunion, is, at best, offending people and, at worst, religious trauma. And at the end of the day, it doesn't accomplish the supposed purpose of getting people to become Christians. Everyone loses in this interaction. I guess I'm trying to say:

Put down the bullhorn.

We Need UN-vangelism

If you want to share your faith, it is going to have to look a lot different, and it wouldn't hurt to follow Jesus's lead on this one. If you notice, Jesus doesn't carry a bullhorn to street corners and shout hateful things to sinners as they walk by him. In fact, if you look deeply at his life, the only people he really gets all judgy with are the religious people.

What does he do with everyone else? He's compassionate and caring and does his best to help them find love and peace and wholeness. What he is leading them to has a famous Hebrew word that sums it up. If you know one Hebrew word, it's probably this one.

Shalom.

It's often translated in English as "peace," which is probably the best single word, but there's so much more there. Shalom refers to an idea where peace flows from complete wholeness—wholeness in your relationships, finances, body, job, all of it. I think it's what we all long for at the deepest level. When you are trying to describe what you wish you had on an existential level, there's a word for it: Shalom.

That's what Jesus is trying to give people. Some people need healing in their bodies, and he gives it to them. Some people need to mend broken relationships, and he shows them that path. Jesus uses his time and energy to help people experience more Shalom.

He does that with empathetic listening. He does that by actually caring about you as a person, about what you feel you need right now. And then he tries to help.

That is nothing like what I was taught. The Hellighters spent precisely zero time helping us learn how to be empathetic listeners.

But let me tell you, that kind of listening actually helps people engage in real, spiritual conversation with you.

Empathy Is Not Transactional

As soon as I wrote that last sentence, I realized that if I was not careful, I could start sounding like some new evangelism manual. That's not what this is about. If empathy is ever seen as a means to an end, like being empathetic helps you get people to say a magic prayer to get into heaven, it ceases to be empathy.

That's because real empathy is not about getting something you want. It's about being fully present with another person, wanting to understand them, and ultimately wanting to be there for them.

One thing people need is a space to think about and process spirituality and religion. Over tens of thousands of interactions with real people, I have found that when you are an openly spiritual person AND offer real, non-transactional empathy, spirituality comes up.

And then you switch into recruitment mode and tell them they are going to hell.

Jk, but seriously that's where some people head with this, and it's not ok. When you use someone's spiritual openness to pivot back into your evangelism script, you've just picked up your bullhorn.

Here's the secret Jesus showed us: it's all empathy. That's kind of what the whole Jesus story is about. God comes down from heaven in the ultimate expression of empathy. But let's not lose our heads in theology here. What people need is to find spaces of empathy where they can be their authentic selves and, explore life and being amongst people who are trying to be there for each other.

We all need that.

But let's be clear: that's much harder than standing on the street corner with a bullhorn. It requires us to be authentic. It requires us to do the hard emotional work of actually caring about other people. But if we can put down our bullhorn and build an empathetic community we have the potential of helping people discover wholeness and a connection with others (and maybe even God). And that is worth a thousand bullhorns.

6

DON'T MANIPULATE PEOPLE INTO GIVING YOU MONEY

"They asked for your bank account and routing number?!" I was astonished. I couldn't believe what I was hearing. I was sitting across from a friend I had known all my life listening to their story of trying to find a church in their new city.

They had gone to several churches and ended up at one of those Giant mega-churches with golf carts to get you from the far-flung edges of their parking lot to the actual sanctuary. My Friend (we'll call her Leigh), had a great time there. The pastor was a great speaker, and they had a small group that started new every week for people who were interested in finding out more about the church and who wanted to meet new people.

Leigh and her husband signed up after just a couple of weeks of visiting. They went through the class, made friends with some of the people in the group and at the end decided to schedule a meeting with one of the pastors to talk about joining the church.

When they went into the pastor's office he invited them to sit down at a table. He took out a folder and pulled out the list of membership vows they had gone over in the class. They were agreeing to pray for the people in the church, to find a place to volunteer, etc. Then the pastor asked, "Do you remember what the small group leader said about our commitment to tithing?"

Leigh looked at her husband and said, "Yeah, it's the same as we have heard at our churches growing up. God wants you to give 10% of your income."

The pastor smiled and said, "That's right, and you know, we are very committed to God's word here."

Leigh and her husband nodded.

"Becoming a member is entering into a covenantal relationship with the church, so we all agree to tithe. All our pastors and staff tithe, and all our members as well. We hold each other accountable to doing what the Bible says, you know?" Then he pulled out a form that said "ACH Authorization" at the top. He said that once they had finally decided to join the church, they could come by and schedule that with the secretary. When they did that, they needed to bring this form filled out and a copy of their pay stub. This would allow the church to set up an automatic debit from their bank account each month.

Leigh said her jaw hit the floor. She couldn't believe it. They never went back.

How I Suck as a Christian

While I've never been part of a church that required an auto-draft and pay-stub proof for membership, I have done my fair share of teaching about tithing. This idea is so pervasive in Evangelical (and sometimes even Mainline) Christianity that you accept it without question. I had been a Christian for decades before I ever heard anyone say anything other than that God wants every person to give 10% of their income to the church.

I taught this and practiced this for years because it was table stakes for being a serious Christian. Along the way, I did my fair share of emotional and spiritual manipulation, talking about how funding the work of the church was funding God's work in the world. I implied that not giving 10% of your income to the church was selfish. I even taught on multiple occasions that donating to other charities before giving 10% to the church was not "bringing the whole tithe into the storehouse," as it says in Malachi 3:10.

Then, I listened to a Christian financial radio show, and the host said that giving 10% isn't in the Bible.

I almost swerved off the road.

Tithing Isn't Biblical

That set me on a path of researching the tithing in the Bible, which changed everything and made me feel incredibly bad for how I had taught previously.

Don't get me wrong. Giving to the church is definitely in the Bible, but a requirement for 10% is just not there. When you look for percentages and donation advice in the Bible, you'll find that there were two ten percent "tithes" assessed each year as well as a 2.5% first fruits offering. I mean, if you want to get technical about it, the first fruits were between 1.6% and 2.5%, but there was pressure to go for the full 2.5%.

Sometimes, you could use 10% for yourself, but not always, and... it's complicated. There's a lot of technicality in the whole tithing scheme you find in the Bible that would make you immediately put this book down and feel like you are dying from acute boredom. I won't go into it, but if you want to look it up online, it's easy to find.

But a straight 10% isn't in the Bible.

Period.

If this sounds like you are wading into ancient tax code, you're right. For many years, the Jewish people lived in an effective theocracy, or maybe more accurately, a theocratic monarchy.

That meant that the money you were giving to the church was your charitable giving combined with your taxes. It paid the priests and the road crews and helped provide food for the hungry and care for orphans.

And, the laws governing these taxes included provisions that provided relief for people in poverty and allocated money for specific municipal expenses.

And to be clear, paying a tithe wasn't outsourcing your care for people; you were also expected to actually help those in need in your community as much as you could by inviting travelers to stay in your home (this is pre-Hampton Inn), and leaving parts of your fields unharvested so that those who needed food could come behind and harvest there.

This information often exposes real religious trauma.

Once you realize this as someone who grew up going to church where tithing was held up as a de facto standard,

you can feel duped.

I felt manipulated.

I remember not only being told that I should give 10% but that occasionally, I needed to stretch beyond that to give more because of some building project or missional initiative.

And I did.

I gave because I wanted to do what God expected of me.

Even though I knew some of my money was being used to support charities I disagreed with and gave the pastor more than five times the salary of the lowest-paid full-time employee.

I gave.

And now I felt like a sucker.

But I Should Still Give, Right?

Eventually, I stopped giving. I felt so raw and wronged that the idea of giving to a church, even one that didn't suck,

I felt like I was continuing to let them dupe me.

But wait, Don't I get paid by a church that is funded by donations?

That's the weirdest part of my job. Though I don't think that donations are a sustainable financial model for churches in the long run, and even though I feel like the donation system leads to large, systemic issues, I still work for churches primarily supported by donations.

I have made peace with that by ensuring that when I talk about giving and money, I don't over-spiritualize it and never ask for ten percent. I talk about our organization's benefits to the community and the fact that we have to pay the light bill.

And that's the truth of the matter.

Nothing in the world is free.

When you use or consume something that doesn't charge you, either you are funding it with your attention (like watching YouTube with ads) or using a service funded, at least in part, by donations.

When you are using a free service funded by donations, you should help support it. But the reason you should help support it isn't because of some verse in an ancient sacred text told people to take a percentage of the crops they grew and take it to a temple. It's because donations make that service happen, and if the people who use it don't support it, the service will eventually stop.What I'm saying is that if you go to a church, you should think about giving,

like a Kickstarter for community

or transcendence

or whatever you receive there.

You aren't just blindly giving out of spiritual obligation; you're funding the service you want to keep around. That feels better.

When you remove the over-spiritualization, emotionalism, and god-ness from the plea, it becomes less manipulaty and more transactiony. Would it be nice to have both? Yes, but too many pastors have abused the connection between spirituality and giving. They have convinced people to give when they couldn't afford it and made people choose between faithfulness to God and providing for their family. And that has ruined that connection for a while, maybe forever.

7
STOP DEFENDING YOUR FAITH (APOLOGETICS)

An old guy in pleated khaki pants and a salt-and-pepper preacher haircut was surrounded by college students. It's not what you normally see as you scroll through TikTok. He was spinning around, waving his arms while he talked, and little-by-little, his polo shirt was coming untucked from his khakis. Of course, the college students looked like they had walked directly from their bed to the quad to see this guy.

I stopped scrolling.

I wished I hadn't.

The camera cut to one of the college students asking him a legitimate question about God and another religion. It was one of those questions people love to ask in college, the questions professors relish, and students talk about for hours in their spare time.

The guy in the pleated pants fired back the most dismissive, demeaning answer that seemed to invalidate their question while at the same time making them look a little foolish for asking. Then he went into the logic fallacies, you know, the way people on cable news phrase statements that make them seem more accurate than they are.

He said, "Either the Bible is 100% true or it's 100% false. You can't just take the pieces you like.

You have to take the whole thing or take nothing.

This is just a blatant use of something called a false dichotomy. This logic fallacy collapses a range of options down to two and implies there aren't other possible options. In this case, there is a seemingly endless stream of options besides these two. Maybe there are some parts of the Bible that are factually wrong or meant for another time or, or, or...

He was engaging in a practice I was taught at church in middle school.

We called it apologetics.

It was arguing. Noting else.

Apologetics was learning how to argue with people about Christianity in such a way that you could prove all the core tenets of evangelical Christianity as clearly the only possible option.

How I Suck as a Christian

We had a couple of lessons in church extolling the virtues of learning arguments to defend our faith. I remember that there was a three-week series on just one of the arguments. It was put forth by C.S. Lewis and said that Jesus was either mentally unwell and thought of himself as God, he was lying about being God, or he actually was God. The short version of this argument was called:

Lord, Liar, or Lunatic.

Yeah. Not the best branding.

The argument goes that there were just three options. The first argument said that one option was that Jesus was so mentally unwell that he had delusions of being God; however, if you look at what he said, he was clearly in his right mind and able to function at a high mental level. On the other hand, the argument said, Jesus could have been a liar and just faking it; however, so many people saw him as a moral authority and even lived with him for years that they wouldn't have risked their lives during his lifetime and afterward for an immoral leader. Then you make the turn into the crux of the argument:

If he wasn't a lair, and he wasn't a lunatic, then he had to be who he said he was: Lord.

And that's how you were supposed to respond to anyone who said Jesus wasn't God or didn't want to accept that he should be the Lord of their life.

And I did. I picked those fights.

I remember being at lunch and sitting at my desk before math class in grade school talking to people who weren't Christians about Jesus. As soon as I could find a way to respond to what they were saying with one of the arguments like this, I knew I had them. I'd smirk and say things in the same cocky tone as the guy in the pleated pants.

I was the worst.

Then, I sat down as a freshman at a table with an incredibly smart senior. I told them the Lord, Liar, Lunatic argument, and they picked it apart.

Because it's a horrible argument.

She said, "Those aren't the only options." I wasn't prepared for that response. She then said, what if the people who wrote down the stories of Jesus got it wrong or were trying to make him look better than he was? What if Jesus was a really convincing con artist? What if Jesus was somehow getting a lot of money from people and sharing it with his disciples and they didn't tell that part of the story? And then, she said that she had a family member who had a profound mental illness but functioned perfectly like 99% of the time. Hardly anyone knew about the mental illness. Someone could come across as competent and have a profound mental illness.

It shook me. I had no response. I went back home to my big book of answers written by Josh McDowell and it didn't have anything about that. It was the beginning of the end of my attempts at Christian Apologetics.

No Defense Needed

Faith doesn't need to be defended.

Full stop.

This entire orientation that situates one person's faith against another is fundamentally flawed and responsible for many people being driven from engaging in spiritual community and thinking that religious people are the worst,

which sometimes we are.

Like, The. Worst.

One of the main problems with this entire enterprise is that it is built on a flawed fundamental concept. Defending the faith assumes that there is one faith to defend. It assumes that there is some single source of objective truth that can be proven, and that's not the case.

Faith is just that... faith. It's a way of making sense of the world that is formed in part by ancient spiritual texts, in part by our study of those texts, in part by our experience of a religious tradition or traditions, and in part by our own experience of life and the world.

All of that is very subjective. In Christianity, the sacred text is the Bible, but the Bible isn't even some reliable, objective standard. First, it was written thousands of years ago. That in itself makes it difficult to understand. It was written before the scientific method, before penicillin, hell, even before the printing press. Did you get that last one?

It was written before anyone ever had the idea that they could have the entire Bible sitting on their bedside table collecting dust.

And it was written in ancient versions of Hebrew, Greek, and Aramaic. Ancient language present a number of problems that, for most average people, are entirely unexpected. For example, there are words in the Bible that literally only occur in the Bible.

If you're thinking someone should pull out the first-century Webster's dictionary, sorry. It doesn't exist. The translations of words come from studying how they were translated throughout history into other languages as well as some parallel texts where an ancient language is written next to a more modern one (think Rosetta stone).

All of that doesn't even approach the fact that these texts are written to communicate the story of God to people in ancient cultures that, in some ways, couldn't be farther from 21st-century America or Ecuador or China or wherever it is that you live. For example, in much of the Bible the culture is one that is based on tribal values; whereas, the dominant culture in 21st-century America is built on more bureaucratic values.

To put that into something with less jargon, imagine you are at a job interview, sitting next to another candidate. You strike up a conversation and discover they have almost no qualifications but happen to be the boss's nephew. In 21st-century America, you would assume you were probably going to get the job because not only are you much more qualified, but most companies have pretty clear nepotism policies. But in the Ancient Near-Eastern world, the exact opposite would be true. There would be a HUGE cultural pressure to hire the relative and train them rather than the already qualified stranger.

All of this makes it clear how so many different expressions of Christianity have developed from the same sacred text. There is not one faith. There is no one perspective on basically every issue, and to argue as if there is a single, correct Christian perspective is disingenuous at best and an outright lie at worst.

But what seems even more important is the flaw that exists at the foundation of apologetics:

that the Christian faith needs to be defended.

It doesn't.

Defense assumes an argument. It assumes that the best outcome is to win or make a person concede that your perspective is the right one, which is not helpful. When you enter into an interaction with the posture of an argument, you enter in with a pattern of thinking that is focused on finding rebuttals to the other person's claims.

You aren't listening to learn; you are listening to respond, and that short-circuits your ability to grow and change. It puts the kibosh on being able to develop into a better version of yourself.

Instead of digging in your heels, putting your fingers in your ears and saying "lalalala," try to take a posture of curiosity and respect.

From Defense to Curiosity

This is making a new assumption about the goal of our interactions around religion and ultimately the goal of life in general. I believe that one of the primary goals of the human experience should be to become a better version of ourselves. To do that, we need to approach life and our interactions with other people with curiosity and respect.

Don't get me wrong. Some people are horrible and damaging, and you need to protect yourself from them. I'm not talking about that. I'm talking about the other 90% of your interactions in life.

This orientation towards curiosity and respect shifts the goal of our interactions away from argument and proving the rightness of our perspective. Now, the goal is to attempt to see a particular issue through someone else's eyes and help them see the same through our eyes.

That happens by listening

and asking curious questions.

That can be difficult for people who grew up in a tradition that was constantly training them to fight. The first step in this mindset shift is to change the orientation of your responses. Instead of trying to respond to what they are saying with your perspective, you respond with a prompt to learn more about theirs.

As an example, let's say that you believe a hot dog is a sandwich and have just stumbled upon your first interaction with someone who believes it is a taco. You might have begun the conversation with, "Obviously, a hot dog is a type of sandwich," only to hear the other person say they've always thought of it as a taco.

This is where the shift happens in the beginning. If you were going to try to convince them they were wrong and you were right, your response would likely take the shape of providing them with the data you have collected from your lifetime of hot dog eating that proves your sandwich position. That is what you have to change.

Or you could respond with curiosity about their perspective.

You may say, "That's interesting. I've never heard that. What makes you see a hot dog this way?" or "Really? Tell me more! Why is the hot dog a taco?" And you continue in your curiosity until you reach the end of their perspective or they ask you more about yours. But that's the second step. You have to shift the way you talk about your own ideas.

You have been trained to fight.

Because of that training, even the way you talk about your own perspective can come off as an argument. You likely were taught to refute other people's points and state your position in definitive or universal terms. You have been trained to speak as if it is the obvious answer for everyone and dismiss or disrespect any other viewpoint in your tone and phrasing. Before you respond, take a breath and try to express your perspective in terms that continue to respect other positions. Treat your own with curiosity and the recognition that

you could be wrong

or at least not 100% right.

You might say, "You know, I don't eat many tacos, but I have had a lot of sandwich experiences in my life. Hell, we didn't even have a single tortilla in my house growing up." Or you might say, "For me, the bread is a big part of it. It just feels like a sandwich to me, you know?"

When you do that with religion, you'll discover much more about yourself and the world. You'll find new ideas and perspectives that might even help you engage with God in your own stream. And hopefully you'll discover places where you have been wrong about something and can shift your belief.

And yeah, you'll continue to think that some of it is complete hogwash (my grandmother taught me that word) and go on your way. That's healthy. But, you will have come to that realization by seeking to understand a new perspective and evaluating how it does or doesn't fit into your experience of the world. You will have grown in your understanding of yourself and the world around you instead of digging in your heels and losing the opportunity to become more than you were at the beginning of the interaction.

In order to not suck as a Christian, we need to stop defending our faith and start listening to others.

8

DON'T MAKE GOD SMALL ENOUGH TO AGREE WITH YOU

I think that the most important tenet of forming religious beliefs is this: You might be wrong. Actually, let me rephrase that.

You are wrong.

If you are like me, you are wrong; you just don't know it yet. And when it comes to God, we must remember this core concept and its implied next step:

God doesn't always agree with you.

That second part is where a lot of Christians start sucking. They go into spiritual conversation or discussion or church or Sunday school or work assuming God agrees with them on basically every issue. We all do this, but it is dangerous and keeps us from important growth.

How I Suck as a Christian

There was a season in my life before I had the tools to do deep biblical research for myself. Compounding that problem was the fact that I didn't know any progressive Christians. I had grown up being told that homosexuality was a sin (more on that in the next chapter). And I held that belief with utter, horrifying confidence. And, when I looked at my dramatically inaccurate Bible translation, it seemed to be there in black and white.

Eventually, I was working at a church that started to split over this issue. I spent a lot of time looking back at the Bible, and it said the same thing. I looked up every scripture passage that could possibly apply, and I couldn't find anything in my English translation to refute the idea. At the same time, I didn't question too deeply because I already knew God agreed with me.

God didn't.

But I left the church on principle and went to another one. I still feel sick when I think about this moment. It wasn't for years that I had a conversation at a conference with someone who was beautifully progressive and asked the question:

But, could you be wrong?

Is it possible that God disagrees with you? They planted a seed (or for the evangelicals in my life, they would consider it an infection) that fed my skepticism and ultimately led me to a path of self-discovery and a passion for full inclusion.

But What If You're Right?

You're not.

I mean, you may be right on something(s), but that's not the problem. Our default is to assume we are right; our brains just don't help us. Our brains are wired to create a cohesive, coherent narrative out of everything, and when we have pieces of information that disagree, it's not good.

The state of having potentially conflicting beliefs is called cognitive dissonance. There's a whole theory about how it works and our brain's quest to resolve it. The super smart people who study this, like Leon Festinger, explain that having differing beliefs is uncomfortable. That is because we have a deep inner drive to keep our ideas, behaviors, and the rest in sync. It should all be in harmony. When there is inconsistency, our brains are in turmoil; they're anxious.

Something must change.

As a result, we instinctively start doing things to reduce the dissonance. Sometimes, the actions we take are all mental, and sometimes, they are things we do in the real world. Either way, the end result is that we reduce the dissonance. We find a way to reduce the distance between the two (or more) things that seem to be opposed to each other.

And that's what happens with our religious beliefs. Most of us have a set of core beliefs. It might be a list that you could write on one of those refrigerator shopping list things. Most likely, it is deeply held and rarely spoken or consciously acknowledged. When we hear someone make a statement or teach something that points out that we might be wrong or that God might disagree with us, it creates cognitive dissonance. That's when the brain's instinct to remove dissonance kicks in. This conflicting idea can't be accurate, or the way my brain often puts it, "God couldn't possibly disagree with ME." Sometimes, without a conscious choice, we dismiss the information and go about our day.

That is dismissive and diminishing to God. That shrinks God down to a size that can fit within our preconceived ideas and ability to create logical systems. It creates a conception of God that confirms our preexisting biases and is ultimately unhelpful as we seek to grow as humans.

It shrinks God down to the size of...you.

I think the absolute best way of expressing this was done by the most holy Anne Lamott (blessed be her name) in her brilliant tome *Bird by Bird*. She wrote,

"You can safely assume you've created God in your own image when it turns out that God hates all the same people you do."

Becoming Friends with Cognitive Dissonance

I don't think there's a great solution here because I think that we are simply too limited as humans. Not only are we limited in what we can understand, but we are also limited by our ability to experience and ablity to express our experience. And a huge complication in this whole enterprise is our discomfort with cognitive dissonance.

What we need is to make friends with that dissonance.

We need to take a step back. We must realize that the logical conclusion of the concept that we might be wrong is simple. We need to learn to hold beliefs that seem to disagree.

Let's walk through what that looks like in practical terms. Many Christians believe that God is loving, all-knowing, and all-powerful. That is a fine belief. It helps us cope with the feeling that life is directionless and horrible things are spinning out of control with no check on them. For many people, it's a helpful belief. But what about the fact that those horrible things keep happening?

If God is loving, why doesn't God intervene?

You could spend a lot of time developing a systemic understanding that explains in neat detail why this happens. OR, you could simply hold all the beliefs without the mental gymnastics.

You can say, "I believe these things that, if taken to their logical conclusions, seem to contradict each other, yet I experience them all as true."

And then stop.

Believe multiple true things that seem to conflict.

You don't have to have a perfect system of belief because you are limited in your understanding, experience, and ability to connect. And remember,

YOU ARE WRONG

about at least half of it, anyway. Making friends with cognitive dissonance allows you to grow and incorporate new data points without needing to let go of other truths you have discovered.

Becoming friends with cognitive dissonance gives us space. It gives us room to think, consider, and process what our life is telling us about these data points and beliefs we are collecting. It gives us space to consciously decide that we don't believe something instead of doing mental gymnastics to create cohesion or rejecting something true just because it disagrees with another truth.

So, meet your new friend: cognitive dissonance.

This new friend is a wonderful partner when you learn how to hold both of its hands. It will love you and care for you in a way that keeps you just uncomfortable enough to trust and change and just comfortable enough to keep moving forward in life. I can't wait for the two of you to get to know each other.

9
Stop the Homophobia

The Bible doesn't say that being gay is a sin.

Full stop.

Also, trigger warning: this chapter talks about sexual assault. Please take care of yourself.

But even more importantly, keeping this lie alive is literally killing queer people. Before we get into this, you need to hear that.

There seem to be two things I can say online that will ensure I receive over a thousand people telling me I'm either going to hell or am a false prophet. Suggesting that God might love and accept people who are attracted to someone who has the same reproductive anatomy is one of those. (The other is that the rapture isn't real, but that's another chapter.)

How I Suck as a Christian

Also, I should come clean here. Among the things I am most deeply ashamed of in my life is how I thought about and treated the LGBTQ community while I was breathing the toxic, numbing gas that is evangelicalism. I will not defend the statements and actions I took, but I will say that I took them because my evangelical church leaders taught me to use the Bible to hate.

I distinctly remember feeling like I wanted to fully love and accept my gay friends in high school, but I also felt conflicted because they were going to hell. I was constantly trying to figure out whether I should tell them about their eternal destiny or keep my mouth shut and let God deal with it. I wish I could say I did the latter 100% of the time, but my evangelically-addled brain did not allow that to happen.

Though there were plenty of times I heard pastors say that being gay was an abomination, etc., there were layers of hate that went so deep they would scare me as a kid. For a while, I attended a super-charismatic prayer meeting at a person's house multiple times a week.

For those of you who are not well-versed in church jargon, that doesn't mean a prayer meeting with a lot of affable extroverts. It was speaking in tongues, falling on the floor, talking about out-of-body vision experiences, and believing that someone's cancer had been cured and that they shouldn't consult a doctor; otherwise, the doubt might reverse the healing.

The meeting was mostly teenagers. We would put on worship music and dance around. We would sing, wave streamers, and speak in tongues. To be completely honest, it was one of the gayest gatherings I would be part of before I went to the pride celebration in Silicon Valley. There was a guy there (let's call him Jason) every week who was suddenly not there anymore. I asked Ms. Pam (the adult who lived there) where Jason had been.

Her face fell, and she looked around like we were in some spy movie and was afraid there might be a bug in the room. She pulled me into the kitchen and whispered while covering her mouth (seriously, I am not exaggerating one bit), "Jason told me last week that he was struggling with homosexuality, so..." She looked sad, nodded, and then walked back into the living room for more prayer.

I still have no idea what exactly she was implying. Was he ashamed and didn't want to come? Was he no longer allowed to go because he was gay?

Did the evangelical FBI, who had bugged Ms. Pam's house, come to get him and take him to prison?

We will never know.

What I took from that was two messages. One, being gay was some sort of super-sin. And two, if you ever struggled with this super-sin, you should never tell anyone because doing so would mean you being ejected from the community that you loved the most.

That is not ok.

Before we go further, let me be clear about some of the ground rules I am suggesting for Christians who don't want to suck.

It is not ok for Christians to act that way.

It is not ok for Christians to say those things.

And, it is really not ok to believe in a God that will punish people for being gay or bi or trans or any other non-cisgender straight option.

It all began to change for me when I was working at a church still under the spell of homophobic evangelicalism. I was working with teens at the time and had one ask to talk to me over coffee. We met a day or so later, and he came out to me. I was the first one.

I had imagined what I would do in that situation for years. I had been instructed by pastors on what to do in that situation. I expected myself to kindly say some of the most unkind words you can say, "You're going to hell." Or find some way to warn him that option was a serious possibility if he didn't fix what was wrong with him. (I know, I was horrible.)

But I didn't.

Call it God, call it the Holy Spirit, or call it basic human decency, but when I looked across the table at the coffee shop and saw the fear in this kid's eyes, I thanked him for telling me that and said that it looked like he was terrified right now. I empathized with him and ignored what I thought I knew about the Bible (more on that in a second).

This courageous gay kid kept coming to church, and hanging out with me, and asking questions for years. Every once in a while, he would ask me what I believed about the Bible and gay people, and I wouldn't answer. I would pivot and say he should make that decision for himself. The real reason I was avoiding the question was empathic.

I knew my beliefs would crush him.

Though I was sure about what the Bible said about being gay, I also was sure that God would not want me to ruin this kid's psychological health and run him off from the church.

Homicidal Theology

This piece of evangelical theology kills children.

I'm not exaggerating. When kids come out to church leaders and parents who reject them and tell them they are going to hell, there is a common response: suicide. That alone should say to you this needs to be REALLY thought through.

I'm going to go out on a limb here and say if you ever discover a Christian belief that makes teenagers try to kill themselves, just stop spreading it, and preferably, stop believing it.

As I have reflected on my path from evangelical homophobic terrorism to loving inclusive progressivism, I have a specific first step I want every evangelical to take.

JUST STOP.

I get that it might take a long time for you to get the conservative talking points out of your own head, but for the sake of these children, stop ever saying any of it out loud ever.

Don't say it to your friends in Sunday School (they probably have a closeted kid you didn't know about). Don't give a side comment to your spouse at the table on your date night (your waiter is at least BFF with a queer person).

Also, the Bible Isn't Homophobic

But what about the Bible? If you have grown up in any kind of conservative Christian group, I'm sure you've been fed a consistent diet of the Biblical basis for homophobia. Doesn't it say that homosexuality is wrong? I mean, doesn't it say that it's an abomination?

No, it doesn't.

Being gay is not a sin. The Bible has six verses that evangelicals say talk about homosexuality (and a couple of honorable mentions).

They don't.

Let's start at the very beginning of the Bible, in the book of Genesis, chapter 19, the story of Sodom and Gomorrah. The basic story is that two angels disguised as men show up in this town as outsiders and need a place to stay. It's getting late, and they are in the town center being ignored by the townspeople. This ignoring is important to note because, in this culture, hospitality to outsiders was paramount.

This value is part of what made travel from one place to another safe and possible. Since Marriot had not been invented yet, there weren't chains of hotels everywhere. They couldn't just get a room except in huge cities. Instead, when you showed up in a town, there was an expectation that someone would greet you, offer you help or water, where you could find a meal, etc. And if it began to get anywhere close to evening, you would get many offers to stay in people's homes.

That isn't happening in this story, and it would have been conspicuous and pretty scandalous for ancient readers. Way too late into their arrival, the two men are offered a place to stay by a guy named Lot. While they are in Lot's house, the men of the town come and bang on the doors and demand that Lot put them outside so that these men can rape them.

That is not about homosexuality, clearly.

You might think it's about rape, which, obviously, it kind of is. But if you are familiar with the Bible (or have the ability to Google), you'll find an interesting take on this story in the book of Ezekiel. It says that the sin of Sodom was not being hospitable.

Also, they wanted to rape them, we don't want to ignore that. But whether you want to look at how the Bible describes this or at the horrifying events in the story itself,

it's just not about homosexuality.

It is about an inhospitable town that wants to gang-rape two out-of-town travelers.

Pause. Breathe. That was a lot.

Let's move on to the next passage in Leviticus chapter eighteen, verse twenty-two. This might be the book that is most often quoted by people trying to be hateful to the LGBTQ community.

The book of Leviticus is problematic in general because it is a set of instructions for the Levites who work in the temple.

Don't get me wrong. I love this book, seriously. I love it because I love ancient cultures, and decoding cultural understanding is an endlessly fulfilling puzzle that my brain loves solving. But solving that puzzle isn't for everyone, and without spending a lot of time with it, you can get a bunch of strange instructions that don't seem to track with the modern world.

Leviticus says all kinds of things are a sin, like tattoos, eating meat with blood in it, or cutting the edges of your hair.

None of those things are sin.

So, what does it say? Well, in the version I grew up hearing in church, it was, "Do not have sexual relations with a man as one does with a woman; that is detestable." (NIV). The version the people use who hold picket signs in front of places that are being kind to LGBTQ people sounds even worse. They use the King James Version, which says, "Thou shalt not lie with mankind, as with womankind: it is an abomination."

Abomination. Ouch.

It seems pretty straightforward, though, right? Alas, no. Part of the problem here lies in the English translations. The word used here in Hebrew is *mishkabe*, and it has a particular nuance. Instead of talking about having sex with your partner, it suggests something different. This word carries with it the idea of "roaming." In other words, on its face, the word seems to suggest something closer to sleeping around.

Some scholars have also asserted this could be addressing sex acts that happened in the worship of other Gods, but there is no scholarly consensus on that front because of the very small number of times this word is used. However, it would make a lot of sense because the book of Leviticus primarily focuses on worship practices and the people in that culture who oversee worship for the Jewish people.

Understanding that there are very few instances of this particular word is important to note when translating. Traveling the distance between an ancient language and a modern, completely unrelated language is complex because not only are word definitions tied to culture, but there are also just different words. For example, in English, we have many words to denote precipitation, like rain, drizzle, sleet, snow, etc. And those definitions can change from one part of the world to another based on how much rain is common.

That happens with sex in the Bible.

There are multiple words, and translators have to map those ancient words from ancient cultures onto modern words in our modern cultures. It's complicated, and even with the best intentions and the absolute smartest people, scholars have to make decisions on random details that push the meaning in one direction or another.

This word in Leviticus 18:22 is talking about sex, but when you dig into it, it is really talking about sexual promiscuity. It's about sex without commitment and possibly ritualized sex in the worship of another God.

Mishkabe is sex without commitment, sex without relationship. It is promiscuity. It's not talking about men having sex with men.

But isn't there another verse in Leviticus? Yes, chapter twenty, verse thirteen. But don't worry, you've got this one. Really. You will already be able to see why this isn't talking about homosexuality. I'll write it here, adding a transliteration of a Hebrew word in brackets.

If a man lies [mishakabe] with a male as with a woman, both of them have committed an abomination; they shall be put to death; their blood is upon them. (Lev 20:13 NRSV)

That's the same word.

We are not talking about the modern concept of homosexuality, where two people of the same gender might fall in love and want to spend their lives together. It's talking about sleeping around.

That's every verse in the Old Testament that people argue directly addresses homosexuality.

But, you say, "That's not many!"

Yep.

And, "Wait, a lot of it boils down to translations that are not nuanced!"

Yep. Then, there are the other questions that come flowing directly after these. What about women and women? Where does it address two men getting married or two women or transsexuality? Where are all the other things?

They aren't there.

They aren't there because the ancient world viewed sex and sexuality completely differently than we do. We will talk about that next when we head over to the book of Romans.

But let's pause for one moment to note that we're skipping over all of the stories about Jesus. We are skipping all the things that Jesus said because

Jesus didn't talk about this.

He didn't talk about the gender of the person you fall in love with or what you like to do in the bedroom.

Nothing. Nada.

He did, on the other hand, talk a lot about religious hatred and pushed back hard against religious haters.

Religious haters don't like to talk about those verses.

Anyhoo, the Book of Romans, chapter one, starting in verse 18, uses this idea of people giving up natural relations for unnatural ones. But just like in the reading rainbow, don't take my word for it. Here it is:

> 18 For the wrath of God is revealed from heaven against all ungodliness and injustice of those who by their injustice suppress the truth. 19 For what can be known about God is plain to them, because God has made it plain to them. 20 Ever since the creation of the world God's eternal power and divine nature, invisible though they are, have been seen and understood through the things God has made. So they are without excuse, 21 for though they knew God, they did not honor him as God or give thanks to him, but they became futile in their thinking, and their senseless hearts were darkened. 22 Claiming to be wise, they became fools, 23 and they exchanged the glory of the immortal God for images resembling

a mortal human or birds or four-footed animals or reptiles.

²⁴ Therefore God gave them over in the desires of their hearts to impurity, to the dishonoring of their bodies among themselves.

²⁵ They exchanged the truth about God for a lie and worshiped and served the creature rather than the Creator, who is blessed forever! Amen. ²⁶ For this reason God gave them over to dishonorable passions. Their females exchanged natural intercourse for unnatural, ²⁷ and in the same way also the males, giving up natural intercourse with females, were consumed with their passionate desires for one another. Males committed shameless acts with males and received in their own persons the due penalty for their error. (Romans 1:18-27 NRSV)

When you look at this verse, it's important to look at what it actually says and what it doesn't say. It says that people exchanged *natural* intercourse for *unnatural* ones. I hope that should make you wonder, "What does it mean by *natural* intercourse?"

I was hoping you'd ask that.

What is considered natural changes from culture to culture and generation to generation. While it was thought of as quite normal and natural for people to wear starched, laced collars back when Shakespeare was alive, that is clearly not the case now. Not surprisingly, how people understood sex was extremely different in the ancient near-eastern world. (If you really want an academic perspective here, check out Dan McLellan. His stuff on this was a primary source for this section)

In the ancient world, they understood sexuality in a system that focused on a hierarchy of domination. Sex was not something that two equals engaged in, but what a dominant person engages in with a submissive person. It's what someone in power *did to* a submissive, passive object of that act. In the ancient world, the will and consent of the sexual object did not matter.

Can we pause for a second?

I know that sounds horrifying and extreme and goes against every current cultural norm. It is offensive and might even be triggering for you. I get it, but that's the problem when we engage with ancient cultures. They are sometimes so different from modern ones that their values are opposite of what we currently hold as fundamental moral principles in our modern world.

OK, back to the culture. And if this is too much for you, skip to the next chapter. It's ok. You probably know where I'm headed by now. Basically, in the ancient world, sexual choice and consent only existed for the person in power and was not recognized as something the submissive, lower person had at all in any way.

In order to have that kind of agency, you have to be a person with power who is higher up on the cultural hierarchy. And, you had to be acting upon a person lower in the hierarchy. Women were lower than men, but men were on the same level in the hierarchy. That meant that when two men had sex, they were making one of the two lower in the hierarchy and putting the whole system in danger.

That was the basic understanding in the Old Testament, and it undergirded the understanding of human sexuality shared by Paul in the Book of Romans. However, there were new nuances to it as well because of the Greco-Roman influences that had come with Rome's occupation.

During this time, Judaism added to those concepts the Roman understanding of sexual desire as being one of the baser urges. The idea that flowed from this concept was that sexuality was only appropriate for procreation.

As far as Paul is concerned, it's a waste of time because he thought Jesus was coming back too soon to use any time on anything other than telling people about Jesus. So, Paul would add to that Old Testament power dynamic the idea that the only reason to have sex was to have children.

Can we just be clear? This power-focused, pregnancy-focused understanding of human sexuality is not what anyone believes right now. And, if they do, basically all of culture and science, and

Every. Therapist. Ever.

would tell them they are wrong.

In the modern world, we have a completely different concept we call sexual orientation. We imagine that you might fall in love with someone you connect with. We hope you will share some commitment with each other and hope you end up as some version of partners in life.

You fall in love with people. You are attracted to people.

And sex?

Sex is healthy and good, and enjoyable in all kinds of forms. That is not how the ancient world understood it.

Here's the argument I want to make about the Book of Romans: It talks about exchanging natural relations for unnatural ones, and if we translate that into our modern cultural understanding of human sexuality, that changes things.

We do believe that people have natural states. We call them orientations. Some people are attracted to people of the same gender, different genders, both, none, etc. With this understanding of orientation, Romans is saying that it's wrong to violate that natural orientation.

When translated into our modern understanding of sexual orientation, it implies that 100% straight men shouldn't engage in gay sex, just like 100% gay men shouldn't engage in straight sex. It's saying, stick to your natural orientation.

Next, we will look at a pair of verses that both use another couple of ancient words you will want to know. The words are *malakoi and arsenokoitai*. The first word, *malakoi*, is pretty rare, which makes it hard to translate because it doesn't occur often in many of the ancient Koine Greek texts (Biblical or otherwise) we have discovered. It occurs in two verses: 1 Corinthians 6:9-10 and 1 Timoty 1:10. Here they are with *malakoi* and *arsenokoitai* highlighted in brackets:

Do you not know that wrongdoers will not inherit the kingdom of God? Do not be deceived! The sexually immoral, idolaters, adulterers, male prostitutes, men who engage in illicit sex [malakoi], thieves, the greedy, drunkards, revilers, swindlers—none of these will inherit the kingdom of God. (1 Cor 6:9-10 NRSV) "the sexually immoral, men who engage in illicit sex [arsenokoitai], slave traders, liars, perjurers, and whatever else is contrary to the sound teaching 11 that conforms to the glorious gospel of the blessed God, with which I was entrusted" (1 Tim 1:10 NRSV)

You'll notice that the word homosexual doesn't appear in that version. That's because I am quoting from the English translation that scholars use and is thought to be the most reliable, current translation into English: the New Revised Standard Version. Let me show you the same verse in an older translation that is still incredibly popular (the New International Version):

"Or do you not know that wrongdoers will not inherit the kingdom of God? Do not be deceived: Neither the sexually immoral nor idolaters nor adulterers nor men who have sex with men[malakoi] 10 nor thieves nor the greedy nor drunkards nor slanderers nor swindlers will inherit the kingdom of God." (1 Cor 6:9-10 NIV)

"for the sexually immoral, for those practicing homosexuality [arsenokoitai], for slave traders and liars and perjurers—and for whatever else is contrary to the sound doctrine." (1 Tim 1:10 NIV)

So, what are these words? What do they mean?

Malakoi is similar to the word we looked at earlier in the Old Testament. It appears to be talking about unbridled lust. This is the idea of someone using absolutely no self-control when it comes to expressing their sexuality. One of the most modern translations that has really leaned into trying to express the idioms with modern idioms instead of sticking closer to a word-for-word translation chooses the term "sex addict." I think that is how we describe people who have this proclivity towards absolutely unbridled, uncontrolled, almost compulsive sexual activity in the modern world.

The other word is *arsenokoitai*, and that one is really problematic. It is always difficult to translate cultural concepts from one time and language to another, and one way that translators do that is to look at previous translations in several languages to see how words were translated into other languages to get a sense of the history of translation. That's where things get interesting here.

This word, which is translated in the less-accurate New International Version as homosexuality, was not translated that way until the 1940s. That's partially because the term homosexuality is a relatively new term in the English language, but that's not all. Because when you go back before that fateful translation change in the 1940s and look at how people translated this term into French, German, and other languages, they all used a similar term that wasn't homosexuality. It's a term that has a direct correlating term in English. For a long time, when translators translated the term *arsenokoitai* into languages like French and German, they translated it into those languages' versions of "pedophile."

So what happened? Well, there's actually a record of one of the people who was assisting with the translation raising the concern. They said, in effect, "Hey, I think we got it wrong." Someone reviewed it and agreed it should be changed, but it just never was.

This should not have to be said, but let me put a fine point on it: homosexuality is not pedophilia. They are VERY different things.

Game. Set. Match.

Digging In Your Heels

But is it, really? Because you know as well as I do that for many people, this level of academic rigor and looking at the Bible won't convince them. Whether they have difficulty thinking at this level or are reluctant to question what someone in authority has taught them, they will hear all your words and say, "Nah. I'm going to go with what Brother Jimmy said."

Remember how we talked about reading the Bible seriously, not literally? Remember how we said that it was essential to recognize when you are reading things about the culture into which the Bible was written? This is all of that, but it's more.

To not suck as a Christian, you have to draw some lines about what you think God is and isn't. And when something someone teaches or you read or see in a video on TikTok crosses that line, you consider it, make sure you don't need to adjust your line, and let it go.

For me, there are three things I think are really clear about God: God is loving, God is gracious, and God is more and more inclusive.

When I look at my own experience and the Bible, I see a God who offers true, unconditional love. Don't get me wrong, there is plenty of smiting in the Bible, but it seems to be described in terms of love. The violence and horrifying things God does is explained in terms of a parent who loves their children and wants to guide them to a better life.

And it doesn't matter where I look.

I see grace.

I see a God who doesn't just react but gives second and third chances, and even when there are consequences, the story is that there's always a way for something new and beautiful to grow out of the ashes of what was past. And that all happens again because God loves us.

Both of those things echo in my own life. Over and over again, when I see people make mistakes and someone gives them another chance, it feels good.

A second chance feels right.

Don't get me wrong, that second chance doesn't always include the ability of the offender to hurt the victim again. Second chances aren't usually like saying "REDO" when you are a kid, but it feels right when I see it happen. And I know that in my own life when I have made major mistakes, I have longed for grace at an elemental level. And when it has been offered, it felt so right. Again, it wasn't perfect.

When you make a mistake, there is damage and scar tissue, and things are different.

But when it comes to the Bible, I see one message that seems to run from the first page to the last. Once humanity breaks their relationship with God, each other, the earth, etc., through sin, God doesn't abandon them. God has grace and initiates a relationship again. Then, God makes a covenant with Abraham, then Moses and the Israelites, then the Kingdom of Israel, and ultimately offers a relationship to the entire world through Jesus and the movement he creates. This seems to be a clear progression of more and more inclusion into the life and work of God.

Once you see it, you can't un-see it.

All of that means that for me, when I see something that seems to exclude people, I look at it for a moment and let it go. It simply doesn't match what I know of God. When I see an ideology or theology that treats people as entirely evil to the core, I look at it and dismiss it because that is not grace. When I see someone preaching things that are hateful or demeaning, things that perpetuate injustice and systemic evil, I look at them and dismiss them because they don't match a loving God.

When I read something in the Bible that seems, on the face of it, to violate those tenets, I either look for the piece of information I'm missing, or I let it go and get comfortable with not knowing why that verse seems that way to me right now.

Another way to see it is that I allow basic human decency and kindness to trump any weird, hateful, violent, or unjust thing I find in spirituality. And, if I have the time, energy, or ability, I try to figure out how to reconcile the two.

10

Stop Asking Kids to Sign Purity Pledges

I was fourteen years old when I promised God I would be a virgin. I was in middle school, and we had a general assembly in the gym from a "sex educator" that the Baptist church had paid for who came to talk to us about the dangers of sex and why abstinence was the only way to avoid dying from AIDS. You know the talk.

It has a little bit of science with a whole lot of fear and anxiety.

One of the stories he told was of a person who met someone on the beach at spring break (I lived in a beach community). The person met a stranger on the beach, fell in love with them, and then eventually had sex with them. When spring break was over, they said goodbye outside the person's hotel room, and the one who was leaving slipped their new partner a note before getting in the car to go to the airport.

After watching the car drive away, the person opened the note and read it. The note said, "I wanted you to know I had a great time and also that you most likely have HIV. I was diagnosed recently. It was given to me by a stranger on vacation, and I wanted to return the favor. Welcome to your new life."

This story was, of course, a complete fabrication and told to us as fact. And I will be honest, it scared me to death. I mean, I wasn't quite sure how you would meet a stranger on the beach during spring break and convince them to have sex with you, but that was definitely out of the question at this point.

Then, the speaker invited us to the Baptist church, which had sponsored his lovely trip to our school for pizza and a True Love Waits talk, where the girls might be able to get a free ring.

I was always down for free pizza with a large helping of religious trauma.

I talked to my friend who attended that church and went. There was pizza, as promised, some church games, and then the girls were sent to a room where they would be shamed about their body and how evil it was and how it was going to cause the boys in the other room to sin. They were given the script they would later tell themselves about how being assaulted or pushed beyond their comfort level was their fault, and they just needed to be more modest.

In the boy room, we talked about how masturbation and pornography were a sin. We talked about how our bodies were meant to be strong and powerful, and we were told about how our physical strength echoed our relational strength and role to be heads of the household someday. We were then taught about how our sexual desires were evil, how we should be afraid of our bodies and sexuality, and how God created us to be pure, and that meant never crossing the orgasm line either by ourselves or with a girl.

It was deeply traumatizing for a straight football player, but if you were not a muscular kid or not straight or basically anything other than their toxic masculine definition, it was even worse. Both groups were scared again with STIs and, at the same time, taught about how

buying condoms was "planning to sin."

After all the guilt and fear, the boys were brought to a worship service with the girls. The band played emotional music. The pastor started talking about purity and being committed to our future spouses. Then, we were invited to sign a purity pledge and leave it at the altar in commitment to God. For the girls, they would get a purity ring that they could give to their husbands on their wedding night.

The guys didn't get a ring because of homophobia

and the patriarchy.

I wasn't sure why people were putting our purity pledges onto wooden stakes until the next day, when the local newspaper had a story about the True Love Waits campaign and showed a picture of the front of the church, where they had staked all of our pledges on the front lawn.

How I Suck as a Christian

I was traumatized by this, but even as I dealt with my own scars around this, even after I was married, I was asked to lead a sex class as a youth pastor. I remember going to a giant ministry conference for youth pastors with a massive hall filled with curriculum vendors and proprietors of toxic charity trips from all over the world. I went from booth to booth, looking for something other than the program I had experienced.

I had done some research and realized that signing purity pledges and getting purity rings were correlated with only one thing, and it wasn't a delayed age of first sexual encounter. The only correlation is that people who sign purity pledges as teens are LESS likely to use contraception during their first sexual encounter.

I finally found one that was a sort of choose-your-own-adventure style of curriculum. There were lots of options for how to experience the different lessons, and the title seemed to indicate it was a different approach: *Good Sex*.

I knew sex wasn't supposed to be good, but it worked.

I bought it and took it to my church leadership, and they were squeamish about the title but thought it was okay as long as I added one element.

My class had to have a purity pledge and a purity ring.

I didn't say anything. I was shocked and probably more than a little triggered. I went back to my office and looked at the research again. I paced back and forth, not knowing how I would get out of it. I returned to my boss's office and said I didn't want to do it. I told her about the research and how it didn't work.

She pulled out a catalog of beautiful purity ring options.

I pushed back ever so slightly, and she asked me to pick out a ring style. I sat in silence for a minute and asked what flexibility there was. She looked at me for a while and said that she didn't want us to encourage kids to have sex (the title was bad enough). I reiterated the data. She thought for a moment and asked if I would feel better if each student decided on their own promise. I said that might be better.

She asked about the boys.

What should we get them that was more masculine? A ring was probably not appropriate. I said they should all get a ring. She flipped in the catalog and said there were two more masculine options in the back, but we would find something.

I caved.

And then it got worse.

We went through weeks of this curriculum and then had a celebration service where students would make their promises (privately on a piece of paper) before God and receive their ring. When it came time for the purity ring portion, the pastor stood up and said, "All of these young people have made a pledge to God to not have sex until they are married..."

I was dying.

He went on with more things that I couldn't hear because it felt like I was having a stroke.

Then, each of the kids went up—the ones I had promised that this wouldn't happen, the ones I had tried to chart a different course for.

They walked up to the altar.

They placed their cards with their promises about their bodies and sexuality on the altar and took the ring for which they had been measured two weeks before.

And I said nothing.

But I Posted About This on TikTok

You never know when a TikTok video will get 10K, 100K, or 1M+ views, but when I posted about my experience with the purity pledge signs in the yard, it was destined for 100K+.

Then, one of the kids in the church I served ages ago (and received a ring) DMed me. They said, "Hey, didn't you do that purity ring stuff with us? Yeah, it didn't work with me."

They remembered.

I was part of the problem.

And to be completely honest, I died. Because the problem is so much bigger than a purity pledge or a ring or any of that, it is just the modern version of the demonization of the body and sexuality.

Part of this has its source in the writings of Paul in the New Testament and in the Greco-Roman culture of the time. In 1 Corinthians chapter seven, Paul says, "Now concerning virgins, I have no command of the Lord, but I give my opinion as one who by the Lord's mercy is trustworthy. I think that, in view of the impending crisis, it is good for you to remain as you are." (vv 25-26).

And Paul doesn't stop there. He talks a lot about the desires of the flesh and makes the body out to be a real problem for us. This perspective on the body is very much part of the culture during the time in which Paul is writing. But to really understand Paul, you need a critical piece of information.

Paul thought Jesus was returning in hours, not millennia.

Because Paul had that as a core premise, anything that took time away from telling people about Jesus was a complete waste. Sex was a waste of time, having kids was a waste of time, and marriage was a waste of time. As far as he was concerned, you needed to spend all your time either making money to support yourself or getting people to join this underground Jesus movement.

He was dogmatically celibate and basically argued that the only people who should be married were those people that couldn't deal with celibacy. And once you got married, you didn't need to enjoy sex and should only use it to keep down your urges (and mainly focus on creating babies). All of that comes from his being steeped in that Greek philosophical culture that taught that sexual desire was just a problem of our fleshly existence that had to be overcome.

And that's why most Christians reject almost all of Paul's sexual ethics. Because it doesn't work, it's just plain bad and psychologically unhealthy.

That brings us back to an important theme we discussed in the LGBTQ chapter. Sex, marriage, dating, and everything in between are culturally defined. That's why you see a dramatic movement across the Bible in these areas. For example, multiple partners and wives are completely accepted in the Old Testament, and by the time Paul speaks up, it's all about monogamy.

You can't take sex advice from the Bible.

Or marriage advice, really.

Unless you want the women to be treated as property.

This is why the whole purity culture and promise ring thing doesn't work today. It runs completely contrary to the modern world's understanding of sex and sexuality. It is taking ancient culture, baptizing it as holy, and bringing it two thousand years into the future to today.

Our Bodies are Wonderful Things to Be Enjoyed

This is the message of modern science and psychology. Our bodies are wonderful, diverse, and beautiful, each in its own way. There is no inherent shame in a body that is bigger or smaller or has part of a leg that isn't formed in the most common way or if it has hair or doesn't or if it only has hair in certain places.

Our bodies are beautiful if they have large boobs or no boobs. They are beautiful if our reproductive organs are big or small or have extra skin. It doesn't matter if our intimate areas are brown or pink or have a lot of hair or very little hair.

Our skin is an amazingly enjoyable sensory organ that can fill us with delight and trigger the release of all kinds of endorphins and positive chemicals in our brains. Our skin can help us connect with the power of nature and feel the earth reaching up between our toes.

Our bodies can transport us into an ecstatic state as we engage in sexual encounters by ourselves or with another person. It can produce a particular chemical during this beautiful experience that bonds us with the other who is becoming part of our world of intimacy and touch.

This is not what I was told at church,

but it should have been.

If they wanted to place a boundary, it should have been this: no one can tell you what to do with your body except you. No one has the right to demand something of your body that you are not okay with.

You have complete bodily autonomy.

And if they needed one more boundary it should follow from the first. You should never try to take bodily autonomy away from another person by force, coercion, violence, or any other means. You should use your body to bring more love, pleasure, and happiness into your world and the world of others.

That's what Jesus modeled. Over and over again, when he encountered people whose bodily autonomy was being violated, he stepped in. He stood between the men holding stones and the woman about to be punished. He stepped in when he came upon people who were being shamed for their bodies. He spoke to the woman who had a bleeding condition that appeared like menstruation for years and said, "You are not evil, you are not strange, you are healed because you have been stronger than everyone else here." (my paraphrase, of course)

That is how you don't suck as a Christian.

You stop the purity pledges.

You teach bodily autonomy

and love of the body.

11

RESPECT ATHEISTS, THEY ARE DOING OK

I walked up to a stage to deliver my weekly sermon. This time, I was standing in front of 300-500 people, and my first sentence made some of them gasp. I said, "I'm never 100% sure God exists. In fact, There have been many, many times where I was pretty sure God didn't exist."

I expected their response.

I gave them a couple of beats to let them recover, and I went into the story of Thomas, how he doubted, and all the information we discussed in the doubting chapter. After the service, a sweet grey-haired woman who sat in the same chair every week made a beeline for me. I thought she was going to tell me how dangerous it was to give people permission to doubt. That wasn't it. She leaned in, lowered her voice, and told me the family secret.

She had an atheist grandson.

I knew what was coming next.

She asked if I would be willing to have coffee with him. She said she didn't expect me to convert him but that he has always talked about how Christians pretended not to doubt, and she thought it would be good for him to hear a pastor who doubted. A couple weeks later was sitting on the porch of a coffee house across from her atheist grandson.

He wasn't my first.

When you are a pastor, and you are open about your doubts, aunts and uncles and grandparents and parents set you up on blind atheist dates a lot. I knew what he would say after we exchanged the obligatory Southern pleasantries.

"Look, I'm not trying to convert to Christianity. I'm really fine being an atheist."

This is the story of so many atheists I know. They are doing fine. And I responded, "I get that. That's not what this is about. I just try to be here for people, you know?" I wish I could say I had always responded like that.

How I Suck as a Christian

When you grow up being told everyone who doesn't share a very narrow view of what it means to be a Christian is going to spend an eternity in some divine torture chamber, you see atheists in a different way. Or, more accurately, you see them in two different ways. First, they are in immediate danger of the fires of hell. What if they died tonight? What if they drove away from the coffee shop and were hit by a drunk driver?

Or...

What if they convinced a Christian to be an atheist?!

Atheists were dangerous not only to themselves but to others, and they represented an existential threat to Christianity in general. When you add to that the statistical decline of the church, you have a crisis. That's why I was taught to either steer clear of them, which was the preferred option, or to make sure that every interaction I had with them was focused on saving them. And I did. But I chose the second option.

I fought the dangerous Atheists.

I mean, the real bad ones, the ones with horns.

I went into conversations armed to the teeth with evidence and pseudo-science and proofs about the validity of the Bible and responses to every question I had ever heard. I would go over to the random atheists at lunch and strike up a conversation to get them engaged in a fight about God. But I didn't do this out of hate or spite. I honestly did it from a place of love.

I was fighting to save their souls.

I am a naturally empathic person and care deeply for people. And when my preacher said to look at the world and imagine that all of them might burn in hell, my little teenage heart almost couldn't handle it. I looked around my school for so many days and thought about the "spiritual warfare" that was happening. I imagined the demons the pastor said were influencing people to cuss and drink and do drugs.

My response was much more emotional than it was intellectual.

I was afraid of them.

And the more I knew someone, the more scared I was that they might suffer. So I fought like hell to make that not happen. Did it mean that I offended some people? Yes. Did it mean that I lost some friends? Yes, but that cost would have been worth it if I had saved just one teenager from that horrible fate.

Luckily, I began to see holes in that approach by the end of my ninth-grade year. By the time I was a senior in my Northwest Florida High School. I ran for student chaplain with a sign that quoted MLK: "Every man is someone because he is a child of God."

I lost to a Southern Baptist.

Atheists Are Doing Fine

Back on the coffee house porch, the atheist grandson relaxed and said, "My Grandma said you told a whole room of people at church that you didn't know if you believed in God."

"Yeah," I laughed, "But they took it pretty well. I mean, they didn't fire me."

Then we started into the questions. How do you stay a Christian when you are a skeptic? What about evolution? What about people who die in accidents when they are young? How can you trust the Bible when there are so many errors? What about God basically committing genocide over and over again? And what in the the hell is up with Noah's Ark?

I had some answers, some I didn't. He liked it when I said I wasn't sure or I knew options but hadn't chosen one yet. And I had questions he hadn't thought of about how the Bible was copied and changed. I wondered about why so many churches focused on the idea of tithing, and on and on.

He kept reminding me he wasn't interested in being a Christian.

And I was ok with that.

Because I have let go of the idea that it is somehow my job to convert the entire world to Christianity, or to anything really. I don't try to convert the world to my candidate of choice, or to iPhone or to a more contemplative practice of religion. I share information and what I've learned.

And I let it go.

A Deeply Mystical Approach

I have decided that if God or the universe or whatever you want to call it needs someone to be a Christian or an iPhone devotee, God will need to make that happen. I can share my life and love and grace with people, but the convincing is up to God.

I believe that part of God is this animating force in the universe. It's the thing that breathes life into lifeless things, the thing that makes water refract the sunlight into a particularly brilliant sky in Northern California, the thing that helps us comfort each other and feel like we aren't alone even when we are crying in the corner in our basement.

And it's the force that calls to us to become more than we are. It's that animating, powerful, personal force that empowers us to achieve more than we ever imagined. It's that force that shows us when we have stepped out of line, and the very same force helps us apologize and move in a different direction.

Call it the Holy Spirit or Gaia or whatever, but don't discount it, and don't think you can do one of its primary jobs: conversion.

Conversion is an impossible task.

It requires taking something that is of one substance and changing it into another. It requires not only a change of mind but a change of behavior patterns. None of those are simple. None of those can be done by you.

You can't convert anyone.

So, just stop with the atheists. I mean, don't ignore them or ostracize them, but learn from them. Let them ask you questions you don't know the answer to. Let them help you doubt.

And then let them go and be themselves.

12

CHOOSE BELIEFS, DON'T INHERIT THEM

"And whatever you put in that plate, by God, will come back to you as a blessing tenfold!" I had gone with a friend to see a famous televangelist at our local nondenominational church, which was trying with all its might to become a megachurch. There had been a bunch of music, a sermon where the preacher had spoken in tongues (non-human languages), danced around the stage, and told some legitimately funny jokes.

He was about to have an altar call, which would prove to be filled with him praying for people and the people falling down by the power of the Holy Spirit. We would witness healings and PLENTY of other people speaking, singing, and shouting in their own heavenly language.

But before the spirit was going to be able to move,

it was time for the offering.

This offering came with the teaching that if you give, God will bless you tenfold based on what was you put in the offering plate. When he said that, when he promised that if you put $10 in, you'd get $100 extra dollar soon, people shouted amen. They believed this. They believed it wholeheartedly. And when I say "they," I'm including my friend. This was my first time hearing this, and it smelled a little weird to me. I leaned over to my friend and asked if it was true. He said, "Yeah, it's in the Bible."

So I went to the Bible, and I couldn't find it. I found things about giving and receiving a blessing in return. I saw something about sixty and a hundred times what you give, but that seemed to be about planting crops, and I could see how one seed of corn could make a bunch of corn, but nothing about giving money and getting a check back in the mail.

That was the first time I realized that someone had been given a belief without ever choosing or forming it themselves.

I had been doing it for years.

How I Suck as a Christian

So yeah, of course, when I was a kid, I was in the evangelical world and was handed a ton of beliefs that I just added to my brain and didn't question for a long time. And it's important to pause here and say that, developmentally speaking, that is normal. When you study psychosocial development and moral development, you learn that children take on that part of their identity from their parents.

If their parents are Christian, they are Christian. If their parents believe that lying is wrong, they do too. That's healthy. That's normal, but as they enter adolescence and their brains become capable of their own objective and critical thought, it's different. It's time they start forming their beliefs rather than inheriting them.

And that's where I sucked.

I furthered this problem in a couple of ways. One of the major ones was in how I taught. I spoke about my personal or denominational perspective as if it was the only valid option. And when it came to religious traditions that were outside of what would be considered traditional orthodoxy?

I was brutal.

In one of my worst moments, I was teaching a class of teens who asked me to talk to them about Mormonism. I have since known several delightful people who are part of the latter-day saints (and plenty who were traumatized by it, too). But when I was with those kids, I chose the most ridiculous part of the story of the beginning of Mormonism to tell them (and butchered it, of course).

I talked about how the founder discovered golden plates in his yard with a weird ancient language on them that he couldn't read. Then an angel came and gave him a magic glass that he could peer through, and it would translate it not into the current English language but the old English variant that sounded like the King James Bible.

I played up the ridiculousness of the story and created a version of this faith, to which millions of people adhere, that sounded foolish. And then I said something like, "Christianity is completely different." Our text is much more reliable and wasn't translated by a guy with magic glasses who found it in his backyard.

Oof.

I sucked.

From Inheritance to Choice

If receiving your beliefs from someone else can be so unhelpful and toxic, what do you do? Where do you start? What if all of them are lies? What if the Bible can't be trusted at all?

Tell me you're starting to deconstruct without telling me you're starting to deconstruct.

When you have outsourced your belief formation to a third party (for likely decades), starting to question those beliefs can feel terrifying,

like you are in the final level of a Super Mario game.

You're out on a plank with cracks, and you realize the only way back to solid ground is going to involve several big jumps on this plank that looks like it might not hold.

I get it. But once you start seeing the holes and realizing you've never given most of your beliefs significant critical thought, you are past the point of no return. You are going to start pulling that thread.

But don't freak out.

You are going to be OK in your deconstruction.

What has happened to you is that you have not engaged in a very normal part of the human experience when it comes to your religious beliefs. In every other part of our lives, we are constantly gathering new data from our experience or learning, evaluating how that information interfaces with our existing knowledge, and either changing our current thinking or not.

While it's a normal human experience that people can start working on, that approach makes most people's anxiety level rise. When I am engaging in something like this, I want help.

I want guidance or at least some sort of framework for doing this important work. Luckily, I'm not the only one and there are several available.

How to Choose Beliefs That Work for You

Whenever I say "beliefs that work for you" on TikTok, someone invariably responds, "So, you just choose whatever agrees with you? Sounds like heresy to me."

That's not what this is. If all the beliefs you find and form just underscore what you are already thinking/doing, you need to take a step back. Beliefs that work for us need to do two things: 1. Help you become the best version of yourself, and 2. Help you find a purpose greater than yourself. Both of those require beliefs that disagree with your current state and drive you somewhere better and more meaningful.

Now for the framework. In this approach to belief formation you begin with your sacred text. For Christians that is the Bible. For example, if you are trying to form a belief around immigration or poverty or what happens when you die, you start with the sacred text.

But you don't take it literally.

You study it, engage with the passages, and try to understand what it meant to the original audience. Then, you try to imagine what that might mean if you brought it into the modern day. That serves as a sort of foundation, or more accurately, a starting point.

And sometimes, the spiritual text says absolutely nothing about an issue.

That's okay because our beliefs aren't solely formed by a text. Like I said, it's a starting point. From there, you consult people. You talk to your grandmother, who you feel knows God like her next-door neighbor, you DM some random pastor on TikTok, and you read books and other writings by people who knew God and who have passed. You listen to all they have to say and suck on the ten year old butterscotch while your grandmother talks and take it all in.

Then, you use your brain.

I know that seems like a novel idea, but I'm serious. We have the ability to process everything and think logically. We can make connections and find the pieces of all of what we have heard that seem to fit together.

We assemble a belief out of all of it.

But we're not done. Because these beliefs have to work in the real world, remember? They have to help us become better versions of ourselves and find a purpose greater than ourselves.

The next step, then, is to live with that belief. The phrase I have grown to love about this part of the process is that our beliefs are "vivified by experience."

Beliefs are brought to life by using them in the real world.

Or not.

Sometimes our beliefs suck.

They don't work. They feel mean, excluding, or like they turn us into something we don't want to be. When that happens, we go back and collect more data, read more Bible, talk to more people, and... you get the idea. We keep working until it, well, works.

The Good News and the Bad News

The good news is that this is just the normal process of life. For those of you who have just begun the process of deconstruction, you might have a backlog of things to work through, which is the bad news.

This is the normal process of life.

It's lifelong. So, you don't have to rush to get through your backlog of beliefs. Just take them slowly, one at a time and eventually, you'll get through them all.

Until one of them breaks.

Or you hear a new interesting idea from a video on TikTok

As we go about our lives, there will be moments where a belief that has worked for us will break down. It will start sputtering, and then we will see steam coming up from the hood right before it all grinds to a halt.

Because beliefs are moldable, changeable things that have to grow with us.

I guess I'm saying welcome to the rest of your life. It's a freeing, wonderful way to live that also takes work. I'm glad you're here.

13

BELIEVE THAT GOD IS LOVE

I don't remember when I learned to hate, but I remember when I felt hate diminish my ability to love. I was young. I was really young.

I was in early elementary school.

The Baptist church a couple of blocks from our house had this program where your parents would drop you off early and they would feed you breakfast and take you to elementary school in the church van and then pick you up after it was over.

I was there every morning early because my mom was a teacher, and I had a lot of friends. I told my friends that I loved them all the time (a practice I am trying to recover as an adult). Some of my friends I got closer and closer to and would give them a kiss goodbye before I left through the links on the metal fence. At this time those friends were Amy and Bee.

I called them my girlfriends, and they called me the same.

I don't really know what it means to be a boyfriend when you are in the second grade, but I was a boyfriend to two of my best friends at the Southern Baptist before-and-after-school program. Every day when we got there, we would give each other kisses, and we would all do the same when we left. My parents thought it was sweet and cute.

One day, we were sitting inside one of those storm drain pipes that, in the 90s, ended up on playgrounds for kids to climb over and through. I was showing Amy and Bee how to let ants crawl on your finger and arm without biting you. Then I saw the legs of Ms. Connie stop at the opening of our tube hideout/science classroom. She leaned down and looked into the tube, and asked, "What are the three of you doing in here together? Come on, get out."

We got out of the tube and she looked at me and said, "Why were these two girls in there with you, son?"

I said they were my girlfriends.

She said that they most certainly were not and asked the girls to go play. They obeyed, and Ms. Connie took me by the upper part of my arm and walked me over to the covered walkway out of the sun.

Ms. Connie said that she didn't think it was appropriate for kids to have girlfriends, but she would talk to my parents. Then she said I was definitely not allowed to have two girlfriends and most definitely not allowed to have Bee as my girlfriend.

I was shocked. None of this made sense to me or matched what my parents had said. They had just thought it was cute and talked to their friends about my girlfriends at the Baptist church like it was completely normal.

But why not Bee?

So, I asked why not?

And Ms. Connie said, "Because, son, Bee is not your kind. You can't mix; the Bible says we have to keep to our own kind."

Bee was black.

I was so confused. Ms. Connie had to state it to me in the most racist terms possible before I understood.

I ran away crying. When my dad picked me up, I walked out, and Amy and Bee came up to the fence.

I kissed Amy goodbye and left.

How I Suck as a Christian

My parents abhorred racism and did their best to keep it from me. Though I have been part of the systems of racism in our country and benefitted from them through the unjust privilege they afford me, that wasn't my biggest area of struggle with love and hate.

I want to be transparent here. This section of this chapter has stumped me for weeks, and I never have writer's block. It didn't stump me because I don't suck as a Christian, but because I feel like this is the one with the most possible stories to tell. I have a hard time not hating people of extremely different political opinions, a really hard time not hating some of the evangelical people who traumatized me.

But when I'm honest,

the hardest person for me to love is myself.

Because I know how horrible I am.

I live inside this head and hear all the awful things I say inside. I know all the thoughts I have, and I know all the things that have grown legs and walked out into my real-world actions.

And let me be clear: they aren't good.

I read a passage from the Bible where Jesus says to love your neighbor as yourself and think, "I hope I can love others a lot better than that!" As I am writing this, I can feel the shame of saying this creeping up behind me, whispering in my ear.

It's telling me that this sounds like asking for compliments and asking people to tell me how great I am, but here's the truth.

When you have a hard time loving yourself, it's tough to believe the compliments.

Sure, you say thanks. You express gratitude. You make a head nod towards humility without being one of those weird people who dismisses compliments by saying something stupid like "It's not me, it's God."

But deep inside you know they aren't true.

You aren't that loveable.

When I tell my therapist about this lack of self-love, they say that spending time learning to love myself will help me heal other broken places. They say it's like eating a healthy meal. It gives your body the nutrients it needs to fight infections and heal wounds. That's a funny comparison because I often forget to eat. So I manage it like I do eating:

I set a reminder to work on it.

I've gotten better, but the gravity of decades of not loving myself always tries to pull me out of the clouds. What I've started to learn about myself is that one of the best ways to help me love myself is to love others.

Because God is Love

TikTok live is a strange place sometimes. You fire up the camera and the connection, and you never know what's going to happen. Sure, someone will tell you that you are going to hell for loving and accepting gay people. Someone else will tell me I'm leading people astray, but then someone asks you a question you haven't thought of in a long time. That just happened.

One of the users asked what my favorite Bible verse was.

It's a question people often ask pastors when they are meeting them for the first time in a congregation setting, but in the thousands of comments and DMs I've received on TikTok, it's never come up. I hadn't thought of it for years.

I used to have a go-to response, but as I was about to say it, I realized that my experience of God at the moment meant this couldn't be my favorite verse anymore. There was an awkward pause as I thought through what part of the Bible felt most true and accessible. The light bulb popped on above my head, and I knew it.

"Beloved, let us love one another, because love is from God; everyone who loves is born of God and knows God. Whoever does not love does not know God, for God is love."

That's it.

God is love.

What Binds the Universe Together

This, to me, is the most foundational, mystical reality that exists in the world. There is this one kind of connection that happens over and over for all of us. It happens with our friends, our neighbors, our coworkers, our lovers, our children, our partners, and random strangers serving us a drink in a bar with our friends.

The connection is love.

It's affection, yes. But it's also the care we have for another human being and so much more. Love offers itself to us in so many permutations, and every time we allow ourselves to give or receive love, it is a healing, spiritual experience.

We have so many options to express and receive it every single day. I was sitting at a bar with a friend (I'm allowed to do that as a Methodist), and the bartender had the most beautiful tattoo of flowers on her arm.

So, I offered her some love in a compliment.

I told her that I absolutely loved her tattoo. It was a casual compliment, a little bit of love, but she looked up, and her eyes showed that this was received much more deeply.

She said that each of the flowers was the favorite flower of some strong woman she loved. She showed me the flowers from her mother, her aunt, and then her grandmother, who had just passed. She teared up and apologized.

People often apologize for feeling loved.

I said, "No. That is beautiful. I'm so thankful you shared that with me.

You have a lot of love in that one arm."

She smiled and said yeah. That's what it was. It was an arm filled with love. I'll likely never see her again, but I'll never forget her arm. And what was happening in that moment had only a little to do with her arm.

We were experiencing God through her tattoos.

Because whenever we give or receive love of any kind, we are experiencing God. We are furthering the work of God in the world. Our loving actions and experiences are literally spreading the presence of God in the world.

It means that the more we love, the more we know of God.

I have found that to be true. Once this became a core spiritual understanding for me, I kept reaching out and loving more and more. I have learned new ways to love. I have learned how to love friends as deeply as is comfortable for them. I have learned to say "I love you" more and more in so many different ways. And in the midst of the storms in my life, it is love that anchors me. It is love that holds me together.

And when I feel the love holding me together,

I turn around

and realize

that it was God all along.

All of the love I gave and received was God being there for me, expanding my heart and soul and giving me more and more strength.

This level of mystical expression takes me beyond the typical nonfiction narrative. It feels like expressing it requires more. For me, it involves something like this:

And then, in the midst of a perfect relationship,
  God decided to make another one to love.
  God reached down into the dirt and breathed
  their life into this new body.
And God loved them.

And then they decided
   that they would create another to love,
   so they laid down that first body
and crafted another from its own flesh.

And god loved for them,
   and cared for them,
   and had their hearts broken by them
and released them

And they, too, had the ability to create.
   And each time they created,
   God's heart expanded to love another
   and another and another,
   And God's heart was broken by
   another and another and another.
Each new each relationship growing the heart of God.

Some of us share God's ability
to see beyond the surface for who people
really are and what they really need.
Some of us share God's ability
to reach down into the dirt
and breathe life into existence.
And some of us share God's ability
to love and love and love.

14

RACIST LEADERS HAVE TO GO

I lived in Alabama for a while, for a long while, for too long really. But while I was there, I felt kind of like one of those colonialist missionaries sent into a foreign country to tell the heathens about God. I mean, the people I served didn't consider themselves heathen, and, in fact, some of them were quite lovely people.

But at the end of the day, Alabama is... Alabama.

And there is every kind of racism you can imagine, racism that I, as a white man, benefitted from every day. I was part of a handful of groups that were trying to work on the issue and confront racism in all its forms and begin to build relationships between leaders of all races to work together to chart a different course.

My church had a handful of strategic foci, and one of them was working toward racial reconciliation. I honestly felt like I was part of the solution. I felt like I was living in an awful place that had a horrifying history and was part of making a difference and moving the culture in a positive direction.

Then Donald Trump announced his candidacy and held one of his first rallies in the city I was serving.

All hell broke loose.

I remember walking into a church leadership meeting a couple weeks later early (which was my first mistake). Everyone was chatting and fixing sandwiches. One of the leadership team members looked to the person next to him (I was just one more seat down) and told him a racist joke.

A racist joke.

Out loud.

Not even under his breath.

As I looked around, I saw that no one was saying anything. No one was speaking up. No one seemed to have a problem with it, and I was shocked. Had they all been this level of racist this whole time and just kept it to themselves?

How I Suck as a Christian

I don't even want to write this part because I'm so ashamed. As I sat around the meeting table with my mouth hanging open and the overt, spoken racism. As I looked at the other people for similar signs of shock, I saw none. I was the only one. I was either the only one who heard it or, more likely, was the only one offended by it.

And I said nothing.

I was silent.

I was complicit.

I made the typical excuses in my head about how he was an old man and had grown up in a different age, blah, blah, blah. But I took my privilege, pulled it over my eyes, and did nothing.

So, that leader stuck around. Feeling no pushback, he maintained his role and kept being awful about talking about "them" and "you know, those people" in meetings. Unless there was a black person there, then he was a little more careful.

But the Staff Christmas Party Happened

We went over to this person's mansion that could hold our like 45 staff people (yeah, it was a big church). Everyone brought a dish, and they, of course, had ordered a bunch of great food, too. We ate too much and had some games that made people laugh, and then were doing the after-game mingling. Everyone was about to leave when I went into the liquor collection room where the host of the party was holding court. I was there to tell everyone the bus was leaving and heard the host say

"Yeah Apartheid is a sham. Why are people still whining about that, they won it fair and square."

I was shocked, but since I came in at the last minute and everyone was leaving, I decided to ask my friend, who had been in the room the whole time, what had happened. It was even worse than the part I heard. This person was a raging racist, and everyone was shocked by the foul things he said. And he was a leader and, of course, a major donor.

The next morning, I went to the senior pastor's office and told him what had happened. I explained everything and asked him to talk to the person. I said there needed to be an apology, and most likely, he needed to not be on the leadership. After all, racial reconciliation was a pillar of the church's strategic focus. He said he'd have the conversation and was shocked to hear it. So, a week later, I checked in.

No conversation.

I checked in again a week later and then again a week after that. I kept checking until I finally got a response. He had talked to the guy and it was all a misunderstanding.

I had one foot out the door by that point and it made it a lot easier to leave.

A year later, I was talking to a friend who was still working there. The Apartheid story came up, and they said the man had been given the highest non-clergy leadership position in the church.

So now, Let's Get Clear

Racism is an insidious, horrifying, awful sin. Except that "sin" doesn't begin to capture it. It is dehumanizing, silencing, de-centering, violent, and many times silent warfare against actual human beings that God loves. There is no place for racism in the church or anywhere, but especially in the place that is supposed to be offering all of God's love to all of God's people.

There need to be clear and quick responses to racist leaders.

When a leader says something racist, they apologize and are gone. They can attend church, but they should have absolutely no leadership ever—like for a long time, but maybe forever. And if it's one of those comments that might be a little off, they need to apologize, and if it ever happens again, it's over.

Every church should take a sermon series and devote it to DEI training. You can use the Jesus story to fill in all the examples, but everyone needs to hear it, not just the leadership, because everyone needs to learn how to be not just less racist but understand the nuances of living in a diverse world.

And if that seems too much,

a step too far,

realize that the system of racism within the church has lasted for thousands of years and has survived every attempt to remove it. Not only that, the sacred text of multiple faiths has been used to shore up its foundations when racism seemed to be weakening.

There is very little the church SHOULDN'T do to remove this cancer from its body. And if you look at the statistics around why people don't attend church anymore, it's clear.

If the church remains a haven for racism, it will die.

If you want to not suck as a Christian, racist leaders have to go.

15

IT'S TIME TO STOP THE CAMP ALTER CALLS

It was my third year at summer church camp, and we had a particularly manipulative preacher.

I had a camp girlfriend who seemed dark and mysterious, like Wednesday Addams. For whatever reason, the manipulative speaker had been preaching about the end of the world and the rapture, and this night was the second night of the tribulation.

You know, because it's important to scare the hell out of children and pack as much religious trauma as possible in a single week.

For those of you who need a refresher, the rapture is an idea that was made up by a guy named John Darby in the 1830s. He taught this interpretation of the Bible that at some point near the end of the world, every Christian would disappear from the earth and go to be with Jesus. This would save them from all or part of something called the tribulation period where horrible things happen like water turning to blood, famine, disease, etc.

So there I was, sitting on the metal folding chairs on a giant porch that had screens on each side. The pastor had told us all the horrible things that would happen after the rapture. There would be famine and disease, and the water and (moon?) would turn to blood. He had said that if we weren't saved, if we were left behind, we would suffer all of these horrible things. And then he said the time is near. It could happen any day.

He said there would be a sign:

a trumpet blast heard worldwide.

And when that happened, all the Christians who had been saved would be taken up into the sky in the blink of an eye.

Unbeknownst to us, he'd had an accomplice sneak behind us with a vuvuzela (those giant plastic trumpets people blow at sports games). He had a second accomplice on the light switch backstage. He was working himself up into a fevered pitch. "It's time for you to get right with the Lord. Today is the day of salvation! Don't wait another second! It could be too late! Remember the Lord is coming! The Lord is coming like a thief in the ni..." Three things happened at the same time: he stopped in the middle of that word, the vuvuzela sounded, and the lights went off.

It was dead silent for a while.

And then you heard the children start to cry.

All of us had been left behind.

We were about to suffer the tribulation period. Then, he came back in a soft voice to say we had a chance to come to the altar. The Rapture hadn't happened, but it was on the way. There were adults there who were ready to pray with us.

Then you heard every chair moving and every teen weeping as they pushed their way to the alter. We prayed and prayed and prayed. I was undone, and my Wednesday Addams camp girlfriend came over to put her arm around me as we cried together. Eventually, my hormones helped bring me out of the fog created by that preacher into a different space.

How I Suck as a Christian

I was steeped in that culture. I attended camp, worship confer- ences, revivals, and in-home prayer meetings any chance I got. I never had to be trained to manipulate people into being saved because I knew it in my bones. On top of that, I got an undergrad degree in speech writing. I was a lethal weapon for the Lord.

By the time I was allowed to be a youth pastor, I was ready to save souls—even the ones who didn't want to be saved, even the ones who had already been saved, even the ones whose Christian tradition didn't believe in the evangelical plan of salvation.

And I did it.

Over and over again.

I took kids to weekend conferences, planned retreats, and preached at as many as would have me. Though I was never explicitly taught how to do it, I knew EXACTLY how. I knew every piece of the format. So, want to know the format? Let's go:

You start light. You're funny. You focus on making kids like you and find you relatable. In the in-between time, you help them make relationships with each other.

And let me pause here. This is not bad. This part is good and healthy and can help kids heal wounds and find real love and acceptance. The dangerous stuff comes next.

You teach them about God, and then, about halfway through or maybe a little earlier, you turn to the guilt. You start talking about sin (especially the sins common among people of that age). You make it seem unavoidable. You talk about how they are hopelessly broken and separated from God. You make them distrust their intuition. In their heart, they are totally sinful, and it leads them away from God.

Their heart has betrayed them

and can't be trusted.

The Bible and Jesus (and what this preacher says about them) are the only true guides. Then, in your next talk, you head into fear. Fear of hell, for themselves, and for the world. You ask them why they haven't done more about saving their friends. Do they want their friends to go to hell?

But you save salvation for the talk on the last night. You've built to it, and all the while, you have taken them through all kinds of emotional ups and downs.

They are emotionally exhausted.

And because they have stayed up late and spent these days doing outdoor games instead of laying in bed playing games and texting their friends all day, they are physically exhausted. They are primed for ultimate manipulation.

You offer them Jesus and salvation and the way to wash their sins away and the way to go to heaven. Anyone who wants to have that shold come down to the altar. Then, you ask the kids left in the chairs to tun to the person next to them and ask them if they need to be saved. Tell them you'll walk down with them. Then you lean all the way in and ask the if there's anyone who think's they are saved but just isn't sure to come down. Don't miss your chance to get right with God.

And they do.

Every.

Time.

Now, whether you get 10% or 50% or the entire room is the measure of the preacher. Clearing the room means you made sure all the souls were in heaven.

And everyone was traumatized.

But It Comes from a Good Place, Really

Having done this to hundreds (maybe thousands) of teenagers makes me sick. It wakes me up at night.

And at the same time, I know that my motivation was trying to rescue people from a horrible fate. I was so traumatized by these kinds of experiences that I believed every tiny piece of this theological perspective. When I thought about it, I could feel genuine fear for the people I knew who were not Christians. And even if it offended some people or made some people unable to be my friends, it was a small price to pay to rescue people from eternal torment.

When I talk to people who are still looking at the world through these hell-soaked classes, they say the same thing. They are the people who comment on my TikTok posts, afraid I am leading more and more people to hell.

Though it doesn't excuse the trauma, it does explain it. And it shows us part of what we need to do to fix it.

Stopping the entire Christian world from believing the made-up idea of the Rapture is a fool's errand, but we don't have to change the theology of millions of people. We could start by stopping doing the alter calls at camps and retreats and conferences.

This might also be impossible unless all the parents refuse to send their kids to them. If we ask youth leaders if there will be alter calls and what will happen at them, and when we find out it's some of this garbage we refuse to let our kids go, things will change.

In order to not suck as Christians we have to stop traumatizing people with altar calls.

16

KNOW WHAT THE BIBLE ACTUALLY SAYS ABOUT HELL

It was dark in my friend's church as the show started. A narrator talked about the choices everyone has to make in their life. They said that everyone would ultimately end up experiencing the gates of heaven or the flames of hell.

Then the lights came up and we were greeted with the scene of several teens walking up to a party. They were greeted by other teens holding alcohol and offering it to the newcomers. The newcomers talked to each other and debated whether or not they should go along with it. One of them said yes, the other said no but stayed at the party. There was some sort of accident and the one drinking died.

The lights turned red and flashed and people dressed in black came out while a deep voice said it was time to go to their eternal destination. The figures in black, crawling like animals, grabbed the teen who was screaming and dragged them through an exit with strips of fabric that were shaped like flames.

By the end of the performance the crowd was so afraid, so emotional that we would do anything the preacher said when he walked onto the platform. And when he invited us down to the altar no one waited. It looked like a hoard of teens at a concert but was mostly kids experiencing deep religious trauma.

How I Suck as a Christian

I wish I could say that I never taught about hell as a tool to motivate people to take some sort of action, but before I had begun to peel back the curtain that had hidden the reality of what the Bible says about hell, I did awful things. I never produced an hour-long show with black-clad demons and a scary voice, but I wasn't that far off.

I was a guest speaker at a church a couple hours away from my college standing in a room filled with tired teens who had spent a day doing service work, gone to a pool party, played basketball and sang worship songs. They were tired and emotionally vulnerable.

I decided this was the time to really lean into hell. I told them that at the end of their lives, they and everyone they know, their friends, their families, and the person sitting next to them, would pass on to one place or another. I told them that though I could explain it to them, that wouldn't do it justice.

I asked them to close their eyes

and imagine.

The first image I asked them to picture was sitting in a meadow with beautiful rolling hills. They could hear a river nearby and see a walking bridge just ahead that led to a road winding around a neighborhood with several mansions. I asked them to walk down the road until they saw a house that was their dream home. Large and inviting. Then they looked at the mailbox and noticed it had their name on it. They walked inside, and Jesus was there, ready to hang out, and they knew that he was there to answer all their questions.

And then, I asked them to let go of that image and imagine a new one.

They were in darkness.

And all they could hear was screams.

If they listened closely, they could pick out voices they knew, and they wanted to reach out to them. They wanted to go and help them, but they were paralyzed in this darkness. Then, they began to feel something on their feet. It was warm and soothing, but it was starting to get too warm, and the sensation was moving up from their feet to their legs. And then they realized

They were on fire.

Then, I asked them to open their eyes. "Now, what if that fire never stopped?" I asked. I moved into a talk about being saved and sharing their faith with their friends and family.

Like I said. I sucked as a Christian.

But the Bible Doesn't Say That

The idea of the afterlife, and especially divine punishment, is inconsistent at best in the Bible. In most of the Old Testament, the concept of the afterlife differed greatly from the play I saw at my friend's church.

Everyone went to the same place called Sheol.

This was not hell or heaven, really. This is a place that appears to be a neutral to a negative experience for people, as archeologists have found items buried in Semitic sites that were to ward off evil in the afterlife.

But the afterlife existence was such that you could call upon those who had died for counsel for help as King Saul does in 1 Samuel. If this doesn't sound like what you've grown up hearing, you're right. It's not even close.

As time progressed through the centuries, a couple of other ideas about the afterlife emerged that grew out of a particular moment in history. From the very end of the writing of the Old

Testament through the time of Jesus and the writing of the New Testament, the people of Israel and much of the surrounding world experienced a series of occupations by foreign powers.

This reality created profound cognitive dissonance around a philosophical/theological issue we call the problem of evil today. At that moment, it was presenting itself in the form of the occupation by what the people of Israel considered evil foreign powers. And those evil people who were doing horrifying things. They were routinely torturing and gruesomely murdering the citizens of Israel. You see it in full display in the New Testament in the torture and crucifixion of Jesus.

At the same time, the people of Israel believed in a powerful God who was concerned with Justice. But that didn't seem to make sense.

Where was the Justice?

Why were the evil people prospering and the good people suffering?

The evil people weren't suffering for their evil actions. They weren't just prospering; they were continuing to increase in their power and prosperity.

Afterlife Innovation Lab

The ultimate solution that emerged from the longing of the people was to consider that punishment might come in the afterlife.

Justice was served after death.

In the first century, when Jesus was around, and Christianity was just getting off the ground, that justice took the form of a handful of schools of thought. There were those who believed that the punishment for evil people was that the afterlife was taken away.

When evil people die, that is it for them.

This annihilationist perspective seems to be the one held by Paul in the New Testament. While Paul talks in terms of the permanence of the soul, he only talks about the resurrection of the righteous. He never mentions the resurrection of the wicked or any form of afterlife for them.

The second school of thought at that time was the idea that evil people would experience punishment in the afterlife but that the punishment would be temporary and, at some point, it would end. Then they would experience either annihilation or something similar to what the good people were experiencing.

Basically, there was detention in the afterlife.

This concept appears to be alluded to in a handful of places in the New Testament, like in the book of Revelation, where the evil seems to be held and possibly suffer until a day of judgment comes and they are all thrown into a lake of fire that symbolizes the annihilation.

The last group saw the afterlife for the wicked in a more extreme light. Rather than experiencing a finite amount of suffering for the finite amount of evil they performed in their lives, they were going to experience infinite punishment for finite evil. This is known as Eternal Conscious Punishment. This is the seed of what most people think of in our modern world when we think of hell, but it was one of many ideas floated around and is likely alluded to in a couple of places in the Gospels.

But that's the problem.

It's likely.

It's an allusion.

It's just not straightforward because all of the afterlife punishment discussions in the New Testament are highly metaphorical. And most of what you think it says about hell is way less clear than you may think. There are two words that in poor, older translations of the Bible, are translated as "hell."

Gehenna and Hades

Let's start with "hades." You probably recognize that word from your high school English or history class as the realm of the dead from Greek mythology. You remember. You pay a toll and cross the river stix and then experience some version of the afterlife based on how good or bad you were in your mortal life. You might get to have fun or roll a rock up a hill only to have it roll back down just before you reach the top over and over again.

That is the idea that everyone had in their head as the definition of this word during Jesus's time. You don't have to look outside the Bible to see it. All you have to do is flip over to Luke 16 and read the story of the rich man and Lazarus.

In that story, there is a rich man and a poor man named Lazarus who sat outside the gate of the rich man, longing to have the scraps of food left over from the rich man's table. Though the rich man could have changed the life of Lazarus just by giving him the scraps, he ignored the poor man as he left his house every day. They both die and... wait for it. They go to the same place. Where is that?

They are both in Hades.

It uses the word.

It says "hades."

It doesn't say hell (unless you're reading a bad translation). In Hades there is a surprise. The rich man is suffering. He is in a place where he has immense thirst but no water and when he looks up he sees Abraham (of "Father Abraham had Seven Sons" fame) and right next to Abraham is Lazarus.

They are in the same place, but Lazarus is experiencing a good afterlife, while the rich man is not. None of this is shocking or surprising to the people who are listening because they all know about the concept of hades from Greek mythology. And let's be clear.

This passage is not about the afterlife.

It's about not being a rich jerk. It's about using what you have to help people during your mortal existence. This is a repeating theme with Jesus. He keeps going on and on about how we should actually help people have a better life right now. Jesus actually never does the thing where he lets everyone off the hook by making this life all about making a single decision that will ultimately place you in heaven or hell.

That's not really his thing.

Jesus is all about justice here and now.

This can be annoying to the fundamentalist evangelicals because it really messes up all the hellfire and brimstone preaching. But let's get back to what's really important, the thing everyone craves deep in their soul: the minutiae of ancient Greek words.

Oh yeah, it's time for "Gehenna."

This word is also one that you might find translated as hell which is particularly unfortunate because it doesn't refer to any sort of location on another plane of celestial existence.

It refers to an actual specific place right outside Jerusalem.

You can go there.

It's a word like Paris or Beverly Hills. It's a place name. A place name for a very bad place.

This place (the Hinnom Valley) is where ancient Kings of Israel were said to have offered child sacrifices. It was considered a cursed place, and when Jesus uses this place name, he is drawing on the idea of its cursed nature.

There you have it. If it doesn't feel like you heard anything close to the modern concept of hell, that's because you didn't. You didn't hear that there was a place where people who didn't accept Jesus in this life were going to burn forever and feel it while being surrounded by darkness.

Those ideas develop later, like much later. They start being formulated a couple hundred years after the events that take place in the New Testament and aren't fully formed until the Middle Ages.

It makes sense if you think about it. At the beginning of the whole Christianity thing, there were only a handful of adherents. It's not a major world religion. However, at the core of Christianity from the beginning is the idea of a just, loving, and merciful God.

God would be none of those things if the only people who had a positive experience in the afterlife were the couple thousand adherents of this upstart religious movement. God sending 99 .99999% of the world into a state of eternal conscious punishment after they died would be the opposite of just, loving, and merciful.

That concept can't really take hold until Christianity becomes a major world religion, and it doesn't. Many Christians in those early years chose one of those other options or a fourth that we haven't mentioned.

There was one theological take that said that the power of the crucifixion and its ability to fix all the eternal consequences of sin wasn't bound by death. It wasn't that you only had the finite time of your mortal life to choose to follow Jesus. That choice extended after you died. They believed nothing limited the power of the resurrection, not even death itself.

Look, I'm not here to tell you what to precisely believe about the afterlife or heaven or hell or whatever. That is WAY above my pay grade. What I am telling you is that making these dramatic claims about the Bible's teaching about eternal fire and darkness is irresponsible. It's irresponsible because the Bible doesn't say that.

So, stop it. Stop saying that.

And above all else, stop scaring children with all of that and using it to manipulate them (and adults) into believing something weird, or giving you money, or thinking that this entire religion is about saying a simple prayer so you don't have to burn forever after you die.

That's not cool.

17

BELIEVE SCIENCE

A man with the classic evangelical pastor brushed-back haircut was worked up on TV. "Science classrooms in our public schools are ground zero in the battle for our children's minds." He turned to his guest, who looked much more like a professor with the elbow patches on his blazer. "Dr. Smith, what can we do about this?"

I had recently been in my classroom learning about evolution and had a bunch of questions because it really didn't match what we had been taught in Sunday School. Finally, someone with real expertise, like a real doctor of... something, was going to explain it. And he did. He debunked the "theory of evolution" handily.

I was relieved and really irritated that my public school had been teaching this erroneous "theory" as if it were fact. I was enthralled with the professor on the TV, how clearly he spoke, how he found questions I hadn't thought of and answered them with ease. Then he mentioned his field of expertise was a field of research called "creation science," and I was all in. I had always loved science. My skeptical brain loved data and seeing how it explained life and reality.

Then they said that if you wanted books, you could call and make a donation, and they would send them to you. And then the host of the show looked right into the camera and said, "And if you are a young person who is going into the battlefield of your school every day, just tell the operators you are a young person, and we'll send you the books for free."

He turned to his guest, "Don't worry, Dr. Smith, I'll pay for those books out of my own pocket. We're going to sow into the next generation." Dr smith smiled. I picked up the phone, and a couple of weeks later, the books were at my door.

How I Suck as a Christian

My brain has a unique dysfunction. Ok, it has many dysfunctions, but there is a particular one relevant to this chapter.

When something seems off, I have to find an answer.

It's always been this way. When I was younger, I'd ask my parents, and then I found out there were people who knew more than them. I asked teachers and pastors, and when I found someone who had a PhD, I would assume they had all the answers.

I hadn't learned how people could structure arguments and twist data to fit an agenda, so I accepted what they said without criticism. After that fateful night watching the Christian Broadcasting Network, I became a Creation Science evangelist. I argued with teachers, instructed other Christian students how to respond to the anti-Christian evolution arguments, and publically debated with other students at lunch.

I was a lot.

Oh, I knew the exact names for the parts of the fossil record that needed to be called into question (a piece of minutiae I have long since forgotten). I knew the location of the human footprint next to dinosaur bones. I had all of the talking points committed to memory.

And I won every argument (at least I did in my head).

But like any belief built on entirely inaccurate information, the days of my creation science beliefs were not long for this world. For a while, I lived in a sort of limbo. I had rejected the pseudo-science of creationism and fully embraced the academic consensus around the fossil record, the age of the universe, evolution, and everything else. Yet, I didn't leave my Christian faith behind. I just didn't know how the two could be reconciled, and it wasn't important enough to me at the time to expend the kind of thought energy it would require. Then I met a person whose very existence seemed to be an expression of this limbo.

He was a Southern Baptist evolutionary biologist.

You didn't misread that.

Southern Baptist, like a church leader.

Evolutionary Biologist, like a person with a PhD in it.

Once I had this information, I couldn't wait to get his ear. I had so many questions, but the main one was... how? How did he keep his faith? How did he reconcile the conflicting views?

I saw him up ahead while walking between campus buildings and jogged to catch him. I asked if he had time to answer a question, and he said he did. I told them that a friend had told me he was a leader in his church, and that intrigued me. I told him about growing up believing in creation science until I was able to really think for myself. Then, I asked him the big question. He smiled as if this wasn't the first time a deconstructing evangelical student had stopped him in his tracks looking for answers.

He said, "I just don't see the conflict."

My mouth was hanging open. I was obviously confused.

He continued, "Don't get me wrong. I know the Bible doesn't say anything close to what our data suggests about evolution or even the Big Bang, but I don't think that represents a conflict between the two because they exist in two different disciplines: science and religion.

Apparently, my face was still registering confusion because he simplified it further.

"Basically, the Bible isn't a science book."

He kept talking, but I had no idea what he said because I was in the middle of an intellectual earthquake. That short sentence, "The Bible isn't a science book," was bringing things together in my head I thought were impossible to unite.

Tools to Explore Reality

This one concept eventually became a core way I process and engage with the world. For me, the disciplines of science and religion are linked at their core. They are essentially doing the same thing: exploring and understanding reality itself. They are plumbing the depths of existence and revealing threads that create the fabric of the human experience.

Science is exploring reality with a set of tools designed to understand the mechanics. It collects and analyzes data trying to answer deep questions as to how the universe works and how our interaction with it shapes it for good or for bad.

And it's pretty good at it. The scientific method has given us incredible advances in almost every conceivable aspect of life. We have cured diseases, allowed for more safety in workplaces, allowed the majority of people to choose to work WAY less than they did 500 years ago, and increased the average lifespan immensely.

But science has also allowed us to advance our worst sides.

It has allowed us to create weapons that can wipe out our entire planet, increase the greenhouse gasses that are polluting our skies, and create global warming. It has given us the personal weapons with which people have inflicted mass terror at our schools and concerts and in our homes.

Key to science is the concept of repeatable tests and consensus. Science lives and dies on whether or not the majority of qualified scientists in a field can use the same process and data and come to the same conclusions. It's not random; it doesn't make recommendations based on one guy in a lab. Science operates on consensus.

Religion approaches reality with a different focus and a different set of tools. The simplest way I have found to express this difference is to say that religion is trying to answer another set of existential questions that can be summed up with one word: why.

Why do bad things happen?

Why does it feel wrong when bad things happen?

Why do we fall in love?

Why do we feel like there is good inside us?

Why do we feel incomplete?

Why does it feel like death is not the end?

Why are so many people lonely?

These questions of morality and the immaterial are answered with mystical answers, often using ancient spiritual texts, meditation, and philosophical logic. Interestingly enough, the vast majority of religious streams also have an element of consensus to them. Except for a tiny percentage of independent religious groups (think non-denominational churches in the Christian world), religious groups develop a set of teachings or philosophical concepts that are agreed upon by some group and then passed down and continually tweaked and evaluated along the way.

Though there is not widespread agreement on everything (there are many different religions), there are some things that are almost universal among religious groups. For example, most religious groups have some version of the "Golden Rule" expressed in Christianity by Jesus in the Book of Matthew,

"Therefore, you should treat people in the same way that you want people to treat you"

and in Buddhism in the Udanavarga "Hurt not others with that which pains yourself."

In Hinduism, the Mahabharata states, "One should not behave toward others in a way which is disagreeable to oneself."

And in Islam in the Al-Bukhari "The Prophet Muhammad said, 'None of you [truly] believes until he loves for his brother that which he loves for himself."

But I digress. This chapter is about science. The point of explaining the distinction between science and religion is to underscore the idea that they are not in conflict with each other. And as long as they stay in their lane, they can be helpful dance partners in revealing to us the contours of reality.

That means that science has no business making religious claims.

And religion has no business making scientific claims. Which brings us full circle to where we began:

The Book of Genesis

As part of the sacred text for Christianity, Islam, and Judaism, it is seated solidly in the world of religion. That means that though it might talk about the origins of the planet and stars, it is not in any way intended to give answers to scientific questions. In fact, using it for such a purpose is to violate its role in the world.

Genesis is a religious text.

It will help us explore our inherent goodness and show us the spiritual importance of caring for the world. It will reveal why bad things happen in our world and why it feels wrong when someone dies. But it won't explain the scientific processes that brought about single-celled organisms or the mathematical models that describe the orbits of the planets.

Those are for science to reveal.

For a Christian not to believe science and act as if some part of their sacred text reveals contradictory scientific conclusions, they not only look ridiculous to the rest of the world, they set up an argument that their sacred text can't win. It's an argument that diminishes the credibility of their sacred text by asking questions of it that it cannot answer.

In short, using the Bible as a science book makes people not trust the Bible.

And that is a loss to the world because the Bible can lead humanity into some beautiful places. But that won't happen when Christians use it to fight with science.

So, it's time to believe in science and let the Bible slip back into its role as a religious text.

BOOKS AND OTHER STUFF YOU SHOULD CHECK OUT

Bell, R. (2011). Love wins: A book about heaven, hell, and the fate of every person who ever lived. HarperOne.

Enns, P. (2019). How the Bible actually works: In which I explain how an ancient, ambiguous, and diverse book leads us to wisdom rather than answers—and why that's great news. HarperOne.

Enns, P. (2014). The Bible tells me so: Why defending scripture has made us unable to read it. HarperOne.

Harper, S. (2019). Holy love: A biblical theology for human sexuality. Abingdon Press.

Rohr, R. (2019). The universal Christ: How a forgotten reality can change everything we see, hope for, and believe. Convergent Books.

Martin, C. (2016). Unclobber: Rethinking our misuse of the Bible on homosexuality. Westminster John Knox Press.

Barr, B. A. (2021). The making of biblical womanhood: How the subjugation of women became gospel truth. Brazos Press.

McLaren, B. D. (2022). Should I stay Christian? A guide for the doubters, the disappointed, and the disillusioned. St. Martin's Essentials.

Barton, J. (2019). A history of the Bible: The book and its faiths. Viking.

Nouwen, H. J. M. (1989). In the name of Jesus: Reflections on Christian leadership. Crossroad.

Bolz-Weber, N. (2019). Shameless: A sexual reformation. Convergent Books.

Attridge, H. W. (Ed.). (2023). SBL study Bible: New Revised Standard Version, Updated Edition. Hendrickson Publishers.

Noll, M. A. (1997). Turning points: Decisive moments in the history of Christianity. Baker Academic.

Bessey, S. (2013). Jesus feminist: An invitation to revisit the Bible's view of women. Howard Books.

Roggio, S. (Director). (2023). 1946: The Mistranslation that Shifted Culture [Film]. ZUM Communications. ACOWSAY, Sweetbread Studios, Quest for Biblical Truth.

McClellan, D. (2023, August 9). How did we get the concept of hell? [Video]. YouTube. https://youtu.be/MQfS2yiVFPI.

To contact Jeremy Steele for speaking engagements,
please visit jeremy-steele.com.

Many Voices. One Message.